More praise for *Spiritual Defiance*

"Robin Meyers has called the roll of factors that have functioned to paralyze the church into irrelevance. His inventory includes ministerial ego, attachment to empire, and orthodoxy that refuses reformulation. These factors, he shows, have in common a love of the status quo and a yearning for certitude. His witty discerning summons to do differently will ring true for many readers."—Walter Brueggemann

"This is an important and delightful book. Robin Meyers is a modern practitioner of the traditional clergy/scholar model of ministry: wise, learned, witty, but with passion for the church refined by his years of experience as a pastor. At a time when everyone is ready to give up on the institution, he eloquently provides a hopeful, helpful vision for the future. Anyone who cares about the future of the church and the world the church is called to serve, should read this book."—John M. Buchanan, *Christian Century*

"While many are scrambling to find nifty fixes for all that ails the uninspired and uninspiring institutional church, Robin Meyers is looking instead to God's holy fools, for passionate Don Quixotes of non-compliance, who are as resistant to scriptural and cultural rigidity as they are subversive for the cause of love. Rather than a Christianity that peddles implausible doctrines, *Spiritual Defiance* calls for a Jesus Ethic that lets go of 'being right' and gets on with the more distinguishing work of challenging empires and changing the world."—The Rev. Dr. J. Bennett Guess, Executive Minister and National Officer, United Church of Christ

Spiritual
Defiance

Other books by Robin Meyers

With Ears to Hear: Preaching as Self-Persuasion

Morning Sun on a White Piano: Simple Pleasures and the Sacramental Life

The Virtue in the Vice: Finding Seven Lively Virtues in the Seven Deadly Sins

Why the Christian Right Is Wrong: A Minister's Manifesto for Taking Back Your Faith, Your Flag, Your Future

Saving Jesus from the Church: How to Stop Worshiping Christ and Start Following Jesus

The Underground Church: Reclaiming the Subversive Way of Jesus

Spiritual Defiance

*Building a Beloved Community
of Resistance*

ROBIN MEYERS

Yale UNIVERSITY PRESS

New Haven and London

Published with assistance from the foundation established in memory of Amasa Stone Mather of the Class of 1907, Yale College.

Yale University Press books may be purchased in quantity for educational, business, or promotional use. For information, please e-mail sales.press@yale.edu (U.S. office) or sales@yaleup.co.uk (U.K. office).

Set in Minion type by IDS Infotech Ltd.
Printed in the United States of America.

ISBN: 978-0-300-20352-3(cloth)

Library of Congress Control Number: 2014039412
A catalogue record for this book is available from the British Library.

This paper meets the requirements of ANSI/NISO Z39.48–1992 (Permanence of Paper).

10 9 8 7 6 5 4 3 2 1

This book, based on my Lyman Beecher Lectures, is dedicated to the people who make up the extraordinary congregation that is Mayflower Congregational UCC church of Oklahoma City. For three decades you have allowed me to wrestle with the gospel in front of you, to be present in your most joyful and painful moments, and to lean with stubborn hope into a world that is not as it should be — helping to transform a small corner of the universe into the Beloved Community. Of all the things that a man can leave behind when he dies, what could be more precious in that estate than a community of compassionate friends? The Good Ship Mayflower is anchored on the red dirt of Oklahoma, but its spirit of inclusion, extravagant welcome, and resistance to injustice knows no single port. Your love has sailed the world.

It seems to me that I have greater peace and am close to God when I am not "trying to be a contemplative," or trying to be anything special, but simply orienting my life fully and completely towards what seems to be required of a man like me at a time like this.

—THOMAS MERTON

Contents

Prologue: The Church Is Dead. Long Live the Church! ix
Note to the Reader xix

ONE   Undone: Faith as Resistance to Ego 1

TWO   Undone: Faith as Resistance to Orthodoxy 41

THREE   Undone: Faith as Resistance to Empire 81

Epilogue: Resisting the Reign of the Christian Status Quo 125
Notes 135
Index 139

Prologue
The Church Is Dead. Long Live the Church!

When an invitation arrived to deliver the Lyman Beecher Lectures at Yale, it might just as well have come with this odd, apparently contradictory, slogan tucked inside the envelope. We are accustomed to hearing it about a king, of course, but the tension it embodies is the perfect description of the church in our time. *Le Roi est mort, vive le Roi!* was first declared upon the coronation of Charles VII following the death of his father, the mad and tragic Charles VI, in 1422.

The surface meaning is simple enough: the old king has died (and hopefully the misery of his reign as well), even as his heir has immediately ascended to the throne. "The king is dead. Long live the king!" Any questions?

Truth be known, this is more than just a clever castle custom. It was the town crier's assurance that not one hour has passed *without* a king. The transfer of sovereignty is instantaneous, just as God's protection is unbroken. The king may be dead, but the throne never dies.

We should admit that the time has come to announce the ecclesiastical version: *L'église est morte. Longue vie à l'église!* "The church is dead. Long live the church!"

It may sound sad, especially coming from a clergyman, but in fact the church many of us grew up with is dying right before our eyes. If not dead, it barely lives. On countless street corners squats the shabby specter of these once vibrant places. Church buildings are on lockdown most of the time, haunted hulks of vaulted ceilings, empty pews, and bygone glory. Inside are dusty storage closets full of idle angel wings, boxes of unused hymnals, and once bright nurseries now draped in cobwebs. All that's left is the ghost of Christmas past. The young say "Bah humbug."

Meanwhile, the clergy are a weary and lonesome lot. He works part-time. She puts in overtime. Everyone is trying to make it to retirement time. Meanwhile, there are devout souls who won't give up. Somewhere, at this very moment, someone has called another board meeting to "turn things around." At this gathering perhaps the Spirit will be poured out on all flesh, and "your young men will see visions, and your old men will dream dreams." Trouble is, there are no young men (or women) to see anything, and the old men dream only in black and white—nostalgic dreams about how things "used to be." Countless churches now resemble museums, whose curators are aging and cranky souls clutching cold cups of coffee and blaming the death of Old First Church on anything and everything except the walking dead themselves. Like Elvis, the Holy Spirit has left the building.

There are many churches out there that are not comatose, though, and some that are truly thriving. But the particular manifestation of organized Christianity with which I am most familiar (white mainline Protestant churches) is like Lazarus.

They have the stench of death in their garments. Budgets shrink, programs go unfunded, and anxious clergy see corpses everywhere they turn. Perhaps we fear the first half of the slogan (The church is dead), yet fail to consider the more intriguing second half: "Long live the church!" It begs the question: Is there still a case to be made that not one hour has passed *without* the church? That even though old ways of being church are indeed dead or dying, the spirit of the Beloved Community never dies? Perhaps we are the ones who are dead, and the cause of death is amnesia. Perhaps we are the ones who have forgotten where we came from, where we are going, and to whom we belong.

So what does one say to the church at a time like this? Organized religion in the West seems at once both lifeless and pregnant with possibility. Ours is the age of the ecclesiastical "in between"—as if one long breath has gone out like a sigh, but the next has yet to be drawn. To some it feels like Good Friday, but to me it feels like Advent.

We go through the motions now as if in a minor key, longing for what has already happened but is not yet fulfilled. It is indeed a strange and stressful time to be a member of the clergy, a religious professional, what Kierkegaard called "town criers of inwardness." We stand around like hesitant physicians afraid to tell the truth to a dying patient who needs to hear it. And yet the longing for a return of the spirit remains, as stubborn as any human longing. We are hardwired to seek the wisdom of transcendence.

Suffice it to say, the Yale Divinity School faculty have not reached out often to Oklahoma in search of a prophetic word, and who can blame them? I live in the epicenter of the Christian Right, a place with more pickup trucks than people, some with bumper stickers that read POWERED BY IRAQI BLOOD. During President Obama's reelection campaign, one fine fellow

proudly displayed this advice on the back of his truck: DO NOT
RE-NIG IN 2012. This is postracial America?

My first thought upon receiving the invitation to speak
at Yale was about the topic, of course. *What should it be?* What
does one say to a church on life support, frozen by fear, and
desperate for a word of hope? How does one pronounce last
rites in the middle of the night while keeping one eye on the
window facing east, searching for the joy that comes with the
morning?

Should the subject be preaching, I wondered, as it had
been for the vast majority of Beecher Lectures? The original
gift from Henry Sage, who established the lectures in memory
of Lyman Beecher, father of Henry Ward Beecher, brother of
Harriet Beecher Stowe, was to establish "The Lyman Beecher
Lectureship on *Preaching* at Yale Divinity School." There, that
settled it.

Yet by definition both the subject matter, and the qualifi-
cations of the invitee, are broadly defined. The lectures are to
be given by "a minister of the Gospel, of any evangelical denomination, who has been markedly successful in the special
work of the Christian ministry." As to the topic, the charter was
amended in 1882 by the Yale Corporation to specify "that hence-
forth the Lyman Beecher lecturer shall be invited to lecture on
a branch of pastoral theology or in any other topic appropriate
to the work of the Christian ministry."

Any other topic? If this was the original intent, then why
have so few working pastors given the Beecher Lectures? Why
has the subject matter almost always been preaching? Granted,
the family of preachers and prophets after whom the lectures
are named suggests communication of the gospel as the obvious
choice. But if the original charge was to hear a report from the
world of ministry by a practitioner of ministry, then why have

most of the presenters been renowned academics instead of parish ministers?

Don't get me wrong. Preaching has been a central preoccupation of my life, shaped by my remarkable teacher and mentor Fred B. Craddock (who gave the Beecher Lectures in 1978). What's more, I am also an academic—a tenured professor teaching rhetoric and ethics in the philosophy department of a private liberal arts university in the United Methodist tradition. But I wanted to come to Yale as a pastor, not as an academic.

What's more, I wanted to come to New Haven with a particular passion for naming the cause of death in the church. This insight comes not from research so much as from a lifetime spent leading a single congregation in perhaps the most conservative state in the nation. It was here, on the red dirt where I was born, that I watched the last ounce of prophetic courage and relevance disappear from Christian communities of all kinds, obsessed as they are with décor and marketing, but unable to take any risks for the sake of the kingdom.

We mean well, of course. We sing our hearts out. We pray long prayers. But none of it can finally compensate for the fact that as a change agent, *we have all but disappeared*. Instead of leaven, we are like chameleons for Christ, absorbed into the very dominant culture we are called to critique and resist. In fact, this is precisely the word I cannot get out of my head: *resistance*. Who thinks of the church any more as a defiant community? Or faith itself as embodied resistance to the principalities and the powers?

Whatever else may be said of the Jesus Movement, it was born in opposition to the status quo. Now it largely sanctifies the status quo. Its founder constituted an unacceptable risk to the Roman Empire, and that resistance seemed so counterintuitive and subversive that even his mental health was questioned. Perhaps G. K. Chesterton was right when he said that "Christianity is not a faith that has been tried and found wanting, but a faith that has been wanted and never tried."

When it comes to analyzing the decline of organized religion in the West, there is plenty of blame to go around. Ours is a culture of hyper-individualism and mindless spectacle. The spiritual life requires a moral imagination, and there is very little left to imagine. The "imaging" is all done for us now in a world saturated with screens large and small. The mind's eye and its partner, the tender heart, are now blurred by neglect. The moral imagination, the most deeply human of all muscles, must work well if we are to love well.

Yet, it has atrophied, or been largely retired by the electron. Who needs to conjure an image when the sponsored poets of commerce never give us a quiet moment, a blank screen? If Times Square, for example, represents the cultural epicenter of the manufactured image, then the sickness of our time is that the imagination has nothing to do. We are assaulted by what others have produced and want us to buy. We have little time for what we produce out of silence, out of quiet contemplation, out of a good long walk to Emmaus.

We are "connected" to our "friends" through the "social network." Our handheld devices have bowed our heads, but not in prayer. Rather, we walk through the world in a bubble of disembodied messages from our approved list of contacts. Emoticons replace emotions; the new meaning of "text" has nothing to do with canon and everything to do with solitude, drawing our eyes away from other eyes. A world of funny cat videos provides a stream of anonymous entertainment and manufactured sentiment.

We consume but we do not imagine, which is why we are becoming less and less empathic. Behold the pornography of the marketplace: Thou shalt covet these things on flat screens everywhere. Thou shalt live in perpetual angst. Behold the way you wish you looked, the place where you wish you lived, and all the gadgets you wish you owned. This is Kierkegaard's "sickness unto death" in high definition.

Other people blame science for the death of church. They point to a new priesthood in lab coats, calm and detached researchers who can prove that pure truth is like a frigid woman or a man with a mechanical heart. Everything will be understood only when the emotions are banished as the inferior little sisters of the intellect. Feeling and intuition, those handmaidens of wisdom, are grounded now, sent to their rooms as punishment for being "hysterical," just like those women who ran frightened from the empty tomb.

Yet science is not a traitor. It is a methodology. Granted, I would prefer that a poet gave my eulogy instead of a statistician. But I also wish that more preachers watched the world as closely as scientists do, and took better notes. Science helps us to understand how things work, but we still decide whether or not to call it marvelous. Faith and science alike have their roots in wonder. Science magnifies the details of creation, but not its moral or ethical significance. Ironically, the deeper we go in both directions (down to the Higgs boson or up and out into intergalactic infinity), the deeper the mystery becomes. Science is not the enemy of faith—only of ignorance. She is like a blind date that we fretted over spending time with until she turned out to be beautiful and then offered to drive.

Still others argue that the church is dying because it is deluded about its enduring relevance. She is like an aging actor, or a washed-up leading man, unable to look in the mirror without seeing what is no longer there. In the social upheavals of the twentieth century, loud voices called for the abandonment of all ancient institutions, including the church, as oppressive relics of what's-not-happening-now. Real wisdom would come from the young, we were told, from those who presumed to have invented the concept of enlightenment while acting as if nothing of any significance occurred prior to their birth. These hip intellectual orphans looked at the church as a cartoon of repressed sexuality, the moral straitjacket of "the man," leftover fairy tales to cushion the fear of death, or the fear of flying.

While there may be some truth to all these claims, none of them can compete, in my opinion, with what should be writ large at the top of the church's death certificate: *The Beloved Community was born in resistance to the established order of death and indignity. It was concealed like leaven in the imperial loaf, germinating as a secret and subversive "colony of heaven," a body of noncompliance with the principalities and the powers. Now we are as compliant as the subjects of any empire, embracing what we are taught to value, and resisting nothing that threatens our comfort, our success, our reputation, or our safety.*

The sad truth is that much of the church today is a harmless handmaiden of the corporate machine, clinging nostalgically to a gospel that is as unacceptable in practice now as it was in the beginning. We confuse performance with ministry, beliefs with faith, and charity with justice. Our demise is the result of the abandonment of our peculiar witness to the upside-down instructions left to us by a God-intoxicated misfit. Christians can survive almost anything, save the loss of *distinctiveness*. We can make our share of mistakes, but we cannot *be* a mistake.

The very definition of what it means to be a Christian must be salvaged now, taken back, by force if necessary, from those who domesticated a way of life and turned it into a quarreling quagmire of noisy "believers." While we fiddle with the meaning of the Trinity, present-day Rome is burning. While we mumble our prayers for the poor, their poverty and pain increase by the hour. While we coddle the industries that ravage the earth for energy and then market death to us disguised as comfort, the conscience of the faithful has been euthanized by public relations campaigns that make us swoon with gratitude for the humanitarian altruism of Big Oil.

Where are the holy fools for God today? Who stands out in the crowd as a troublemaker for justice? Where can we find the spiritual contrarian, unplugged and unmoved by the choreographed hysteria of celebrity culture? Where do we find real wisdom in the age of the blog, where everyone with an opinion can self-publish, where authors presume not to need editors in a worldwide web of intellectual autoeroticism?

The sad truth is that to help the American church "grow" we have dressed it in the uniform of Western culture. We have taught its leaders to be entrepreneurs, and to fret more about parking spaces than about peace and justice. We sing familiar hymns, but the lyrics fall on deaf ears. We recite creeds in worship that move no one, while others have decided they cannot speak them aloud in good conscience. In short, countless communities of faith are engaged in a charade on Sunday morning. The pews are full of pretenders.

The easiest thing would be to give up, of course, to disappear, to slide happily into retirement while telling the same tired old stories in the pulpit about walking with Jesus on the beach but seeing only one set of footprints in the sand. The real enemies of the church are found inside its walls. Sadly, the clergy shop as frantically as anyone at Christmastime, instead of warning people that the nativity is really a spiritual apocalypse. We commend praying for our enemies without confessing that the idea is more absurd and un-American than soccer. We cheer Jesus the Gentile lover while funding allies who are Gentile haters. We read the Sermon on the Mount as if it came from the back of a cereal box.

So let this be the subject of my Beecher Lectures and book: faith as *resistance:* to ego, to orthodoxy, and last, but not least, to empire. Let it be known that this cry, "The church is dead, love live the church!" comes from a pastor, not from an evangelical atheist. It comes from a minister who is just as susceptible to the comforts of capitulation as the next man. Just as eager to make it to retirement with more than enough to live on. Just as tempted by the illusions of the prophetic so long as it costs me nothing. Just as egocentric and insatiable as are most clergy in search of affirmation. Just as happy to enjoy the benefits of empire, to mouth the mental laziness of orthodoxy, and to succumb to the seductions of "praise without practice" that afflict so many men and women of God.

There will be no recovery of the Beloved Community until we resist taking ourselves too seriously (ego); until we resist taking the purity of "right beliefs" and "right worship" too seriously (orthodoxy); and until we resist taking our marching orders from the powers that be (empire) too seriously. Instead, we can renew the church but one way—by taking the "narrow way" much more seriously. "And blessed is he who takes no offense at me."

Note to the Reader

The Lyman Beecher Lectures are rhetorical events. They are created for the ear, not for the eye. They are oral/aural moments, not textual ones. The best way to experience them is to listen to them, not to read them. Therefore, to expand them into a book is to change their character in unavoidable ways. To freeze them on the page is to steal the singular and irreplaceable moment when a speaker is present with an audience in a moment of time.

Gone is the power of the human voice casting out words in the presence of attentive and expectant faces. Gone too is the laughter, the sound of "amen," and the power of dialectic. Gone is the real-time crackle of call and response. Gone, in other words, is human communication in its native form: the world of *sound*. Gone also is the gorgeous music that came before, the prayers that lifted us to the moment, and the glorious October light that bathed the solemnity of the Marquand Chapel.

I apologize in advance that I am helpless to recover any of this for the reader, and ask for your understanding in what strikes all preachers as a downgrade. The 2013–14 Beecher Lectures were the first ever to be simulcast, however, allowing anyone with a computer and Internet access to hear them live. They were also recorded, produced, and posted to YouTube, where they may be listened to as originally delivered. I am grateful to Jared Gilbert, Director of Communications and Media at Yale Divinity School, for his outstanding work.

For this book, the main title has been changed, and each of the lectures has been expanded by a third. There are additional source citations added, and a prologue and epilogue to help frame the contents for the reader. I remain deeply grateful to the Yale Divinity School faculty for their gracious invitation to give these renowned lectures. I am further indebted to Yale University Press, my editor Jennifer Banks, her editorial assistant Heather Gold, and editors Joyce Ippolito and Margaret Otzel, for the added privilege and challenge of turning them into a book.

1

Undone

Faith as Resistance to Ego

The human ego prefers anything, just about anything, to falling, or changing, or dying. The ego is that part of you that loves the status quo—even when it's not working. It attaches to past and present and fears the future.

—*Richard Rohr*

Audacity comes easily to most preachers. Not because we are a naturally arrogant lot, or have world-saving delusions of grandeur, but because we are asked to perform an audacious act every Sunday—to stand before our congregations and presume to tell strangers the secrets of their own hearts, even when we have yet to admit to all of our own. They listen politely and patiently, even when we don't know what we are talking about, and a deadly illusion sets

1

in—that we *do* know what we are talking about. The ego is such a beast.

For example, before I even opened the envelope from Yale, I thought to myself, *I'll bet that's an invitation to give the Beecher Lectures*. This shameful little game is how the ego works, if we are honest. Because if it is not the invitation, you can pretend that you were only kidding. But if it is, then you can appear to be clairvoyant. What I had not counted on, however, was what actually happened. When I opened the letter and read it, I felt *undone*—in the way that Kierkegaard says that faith should undo us. Disorient us. Make us feel at first as if we are falling.

Let me begin with the obvious. It is one thing to pretend to be smarter than you really are in Oklahoma. It is quite another thing to do so at Yale. Because, really, what do I have to say to anyone at Yale that is worth their time? *What happens*, I asked myself, *if the expectations of the audience exceed the capacity of the speaker? What if the ego is no match for the angst?* What do any of us have to say when it isn't good enough just to be clever, or to sound appropriately theological, or to be what William Sloane Coffin, Jr., called "a mad prophet decrying the hypocrisies of our time"? It reminds me of the man who went to see his therapist one day and began by saying, "Doc, I feel miserable." The therapist responded, "Good, can you stay with the feeling?"

For all the months leading up to the lectures, I awakened every morning with a nagging question: *How do I stay with the feeling of being undone—instead of just covering it up with words?* How might I speak in such a way that the illusions of our cleverness, our self-sufficiency, even our academic grandeur might also be undone? Broken down. Disassembled. Scattered like a covey of quail—and then startled by grace before those feathers hit the ground.

A nervous speaker is the rule. A crowd made anxious by what they are hearing is the exception. And to be honest, I'd rather not think of my words as just a rhetorical performance that is scored like a diving contest (where I speak and then the audience, the judges, hold up numbers). Rather, God willing, I'd like for all of us to lean into the wind of something that *really matters*—something uncomfortably outside the realm of cleverness and erudition.

My hope is that the real audience might be wider than clergy or those who train them. That indeed the whole church might have "ears to hear." That each of us might see our own reflection in the excesses of the ego; might confess that we all know the temptations of orthodoxy; might confront together with intellectual honesty the seductions of empire. It is possible, after all, that even at Yale there is no amount of intellectual firepower that can fully compensate for human folly. Having spent half my life in the world of academia, I know this to be true: we can be so smart and so lost.

I should be talking about preaching, of course, like my colleagues before me. Preaching has always been fundamental to me, indeed something closer to an obsession. But I came to Yale to talk about someone else. It is something that concerns every spiritual community on earth and has profound implications for the future of the life of faith. I came not as an outsider, but as the pastor of the same progressive congregation for three decades, struggling to reclaim Christianity as a way of life, not a system of creeds and doctrines demanding total agreement.

In my native Oklahoma, reddest of the red states, one can be either a Christian or a Democrat. To be both, however, is inconceivable. Or, as we like to say in Oklahoma, "peculiar." I am a child of the high plains, raised beneath that infinite horizon and parented by a pioneering class of people possessed of a kind of "hybrid vitality." Mine is the land of Woody Guthrie, the end of the Trail of Tears, and the Dust Bowl that turned the sky black at high noon (as author Timothy Egan put it, "the worst hard time").

I was born in Oklahoma City, delivered by a doctor who would one day become a member of my church. Had he known all those years ago, he could have slapped my bottom and said, "That's my pastor!" The squealing baby in his gloved hands would one day eulogize his first wife and then place a ring in his aging hand to pronounce him married to his second. Life is truly an astonishing and grace-full circle.

Raised in the white-bread Protestant mecca of Wichita, Kansas, a product of public schools, I spent a happy childhood in a bungalow parsonage right next door to a non-instrumental Church of Christ that my father served as pastor. Called Riverside (not to be confused with that cathedral on the banks of the Hudson in New York City), it was a small, middle-class congregation full of plumbers and carpenters and schoolteachers—all of them looking for the answer to every conceivable question somewhere in the pages of the New Testament. "Where the Bible speaks, we speak," they would say. "Where the Bible is silent, we are silent." I had no idea at the time how many topics that meant we could not talk about.

Nor little did I know as a child that my father was actually in the process of leaving the Church of Christ, only to raise a son who would one day serve the *United* Church of Christ, two names that are so similar as to be constantly confused in my neck of the woods. Here is how the conversation goes:

"What church do you serve?"
"Mayflower Congregational United Church of Christ," I reply.

"Oh, Church of Christ? So you don't have any musical
instruments in worship?"
"No, *United* Church of Christ. UCC."
[Long pause] . . . "Oh, the gay church."

Well, not exactly. But I do serve a church that is very intentional about the practice of extending an "extravagant welcome."
It can often seem strange in a world of hyper-polemical rhetoric
and identity politics that the challenge of loving one another
waits on something much more basic: *understanding one another.* When it comes to the Beloved Community, the ego must
give way to something more powerful than image or ambition.

So let's begin with the help of poetry. Each chapter in this
book is framed on three different poems written by the extraordinary Polish poet Anna Kamieńska. Taken from a collection
of her poems entitled *Astonishments*, the first offering is meant
to begin our conversation about the ego as both a threat to, and
yet in some indentured form, essential to our lives together in
the community of faith.

I could have picked a text from scripture, of course. This
is my life's work. But I am a great believer that ministers don't
read enough poetry, and people in church don't hear enough
of it read in the sanctuary. I also believe that theologians could
learn a lot from poets, especially about silence.

The poem is entitled "Transformation."

To be transformed
to turn yourself inside out like a glove
to spin like a planet
to thread yourself through yourself
so that each day penetrates each night
so that each word runs to the other side of truth

so that each verse comes out of itself
so that each face leaning on a hand
sweats into the skin of the palm

So that this pen
changes into pure silence
I wanted to say into love

To fall off a horse
to smear your face with dust
to be blinded
to lift yourself
and allow yourself to be led
like blind Saul
to Damascus[1]

To begin, let me explain myself when it comes to both the
theme of faith as resistance, and the use of the word "undone."
For a variety of reasons I hope to make clear, after three decades
of parish ministry I have come to believe that of all the reasons
given for the decline of the church in our time, far too much
attention has been given to how successfully or unsuccessfully
the church markets a culturally acceptable form of spirituality,
while far too little has been given to the body of Christ as a
community of resistance.

What Do You Mean by Resistance?

To be clear, by resistance I mean that the church of Jesus
Christ should be, as it once was, an "embodied force opposed,"
a beloved community of defiance, a joyful but resilient colony
of dissenters from the forces of death—both physical and
spiritual—that destroy and marginalize creation. The assumed

premise here is that compliance with the unacceptable, even through apathy or indifference, is a sin. The body of Christ was born to resist in love all that is the enemy of love. This cannot happen, however, until human beings are themselves freed from the illusions that afflict us—that is, until we are "undone."

In the evangelical community, the work of Jesus is often described as "saving souls," and salvation is defined as our response to a belief system. It is sustained by the illusion that intellectual assent to theological propositions is inherently redemptive. Those who hold the power of orthodoxy wield it over those who are "lost," and the image that comes to mind is that of a true believer astride a horse. Faith as resistance, on the other hand, requires that, in the words of the poet, we *fall off that horse* and are temporarily blinded. What we cannot see after this "fall" is life itself as it once appeared to us clouded by illusion. Having thus been "undone," we are committed to the "undoing" of others. This means that we resist the idea that we are "saving" souls, and think instead of "restoring" them.

By resistance I do not mean simply to be a drag on something, as when resistors are used to regulate the flow of electricity. And neither do I mean by resistance only that we should protest more by marching in the streets—although this may sometimes be called for. Nor do I mean that the body of Christ should be more obstinate or cranky, a kind of cultural contrarian, complaining about how "nothing is like it used to be" (Why can't we sing the old hymns, and where have all the young people gone?). *I'm talking instead about resistance as a form of direct or indirect action opposing anything in the dominant culture that brings death and indignity to any member of the human family, or to creation itself.*

Such spiritual resistance can be either overt or covert, but it must always be a self-conscious and intentional decision to obey, as a disciple, the radical demands of the kingdom of God. By definition, we are a community that lives to honor our inheritance (that is, to remember), but we are also called to shape the future through hope, to bend the arc of history toward justice, as Dr. King would say. Memory and hope are the two strongest forces in human life. So as a community of faith, we embrace our narrative of origin (the scriptures) in order to reshape the narrative of our destiny.

Or to use a modern analogy, consider the common experience of watching previews of coming attractions at a movie theater. Hollywood uses them to whet our appetite for the full feature. In the same way, the church must also provide "embodied previews," real-life "trailers" (sneak peeks, if you will), of what the coming reign of God will look like until the full feature arrives. Or to put this in the lingo of cinema, our churches often look and feel like a *sequel*, when they ought to look and feel more like a *prequel*.

Worship can even be performed as a collective act of community resistance, and it can be theatrical, in the best sense of the word, akin to what Anna Carter Florence called the "Repertory Church."[2] We are engaged in a divine drama, acting out the gospel on an ecclesiastical stage. Being "in character" means more than just assuming an alternative identity. It means *becoming* that vision of creation healed that is the dream of the prophets. Contrary to the seductions of ego, we resist "acting for acting's sake," and work instead to create a scene that transcends good reviews, curtain calls, or applause. Rather, its purpose is to give us a glimpse of what will come after, not just what has come before.

This is much harder than it sounds, of course. In the religion business, we are better at being sentimental than we are at being hopeful. And ministry is a career, which means that the clergy are trained to please the various constituencies that will advance their career. Yet we do this at the risk of forgetting that our first obligation is to please only the One who called us, to speak in love nothing more or less than the truth that Love has taught us—even, and perhaps especially, when such a word challenges the status quo.

OK, that's lovely, you say? Sounds just like something you would expect to hear from a social gospel preacher. But here's the catch. None of it can happen until we are undone. Or as the poet puts it, until "we fall off [our] horse." In the church, as in life itself, the rule of entropy still applies. Things fall apart before they are put back together. *Disorientation* precedes *reorientation*. Not just for the clergy or the congregation, but indeed for all human beings, families, even nations—they all tumble sooner or later from that saddle of illusion. Only then are we vulnerable enough to hear voices; only then are we blinded enough to be led. Only then are we weak enough to be made strong.

The word "undone" comes by way of Søren Kierkegaard, and with the help of Fred Craddock. Craddock's 1978 Beecher Lectures, "Overhearing the Gospel," explored the notion of indirect communication in preaching. By way of Kierkegaard, Craddock gave us all a simple, but unforgettable metaphor for approaching the text with both humility and expectation. We would do well to remember, Craddock said, that by definition we approach the text as distant strangers. All of us are on our knees, as it were, *listening through a keyhole to an ancient conversation not intended for us.*

Not a word of the Bible is written to any of us, rendering the mantra "the Bible says!" nonsense. The Bible *said*, and now we *say*. Our posture is one of overhearing what Kierkegaard thought of as a "conversation" between God and God's people. The preacher's task is to listen first, and then to make a report, not just on what God *was* up to, but on what God might *still* be up to.[3]

Aristotle believed that the most effective communicators were "audience centered," but preaching is inherently a public performance, and ministers are called (or not called) to churches largely on how well they preach. Is it any wonder, then, that the ego of the minister, or any communicator for that matter, becomes the most formidable obstacle of all in telling the story? It is not our story we are telling, of course, but without passion there is no persuasion, and there is no passion without personal involvement. So for clergy the struggle is always to find a balance between intimacy and distance. How close does one stand to the gospel, at the risk of casting one's shadow over it, and how far away does one stand before it becomes a kind of sentimental mirage, shimmering safely in the distance but devoid of living water?

Is Ministry a Calling or a Career?

In the vernacular of church we are fond of saying that ministers are "called" to their vocation. One presumes this means called by God, but it's often hard to tell exactly where the voice is coming from. In seminary, one of my colleagues claimed that he heard the voice of God coming from his stereo speakers, bidding him to enter the ministry. I was tempted in a moment of irreverence to ask whether the voice had more bass than treble, but to be honest I was almost envious. No clear voice had called me (mostly it was Bob Dylan coming out of my speakers), and so I wondered if I was in the right place, or had the wrong kind of stereo.

Many of us are familiar with Frederick Buechner's wise words about the ministry as sacred vocation, and his warnings as well:

It comes from the Latin *vocare*, to call, and means the work a man is called to by God. There are all different kinds of voices calling you to all different kinds of work, and the problem is to find out which is the voice of God rather than of Society, say, or the Super-ego, or Self-interest. By and large a good rule for finding out is this. The kind of work God usually calls you to is the kind of work (*a*) that you need most to do and (*b*) that the world most needs to have done. If you really get a kick out of your work, you've presumably met requirement (*a*), but if your work is writing TV deodorant commercials, the chances are you've missed requirement (*b*). On the other hand, if your work is being a doctor in a leper colony, you have probably met requirement (*b*), but if most of the time you're bored and depressed by it, the chances are you have not only bypassed (*a*) but probably aren't helping your patients much either. Neither the hair shirt nor the soft berth will do. The place God calls you to is the place where your deep gladness and the world's deep hunger meet.[4]

That beautiful last line still rings in the ear of many clergy, "the place where your deep gladness and the world's deep hunger meet." In reality, however, the deep hunger seems to have overwhelmed the deep gladness. Or perhaps the daily grind of parish programs and institutional goals has drained the well of joy. The great Luther theologian Joseph Sittler called it the "maceration of the minister."

By this rather startling phrase he meant to drive home the simple truth that clergy can be "chopped into small pieces" by trading a calling for a career. Once in the classroom they were on fire with ideas like *basilica tou Theu*, but now the working pastor unplugs toilets, frets over shrinking budgets, and imagines conspiracies where they don't exist, while ignoring the secret pain of parishioners that is all too real.

Take note of the books that a seminary student is reading in graduate school. Then check back to see what has covered them up on the desk of a working pastor. The difference is both striking and sad. As Sittler put it (pre–inclusive language): "Visit the man some years later in what the man still calls inexactly his study and one is more than likely to find him accompanied by the same volumes he took with him from his student room. And filed on top of even these are mementos of what he is presently concerned with: a roll of blueprints, a file of negotiations between the parish, the bank, and the Board of Missions, samples of asphalt tile, and a plumber's estimate."[5]

This long and winding road by which a prophet becomes an entrepreneur is littered with small compromises. Ministers are ordained to an Office, but too often end up running an office. What drives this demotion is the self-image of the minister, and the daily tension between the gospel's brutal candor and the minister's equivocation in service to admiration and promotion. Inevitably, in order to see oneself as "successful" in the marketplace of the ministry, one must gradually lay aside candor in favor of a kind of pragmatic sincerity. Hence we have a church full of "sincere" clergy who cannot understand why "doing no harm" so often excludes the possibility of doing any good.

The overly cautious preacher ends up like the boy who cried wolf. Repeated deception ultimately erodes credibility. Offending no one in the pulpit virtually guarantees that you will also inspire no one, because mediocrity is the devil's bargain. The preacher who will not risk the wrath of a listener for the sake of the gospel gradually comes to realize that lack of candor increases comfort while simultaneously undermining power. Soon the fateful day arrives when truth must be spoken to power. But alas, there is neither truth nor power to be found.

Oh Wretched Man That I Am!

Not to sound old-fashioned about it, but first we must *repent*. By repent I mean to "turn around," as known most fully in the verb form of the Greek *metanoia*—to "turn around" or "turn back"—even in classical Greek to "repel an enemy." That enemy, however, is more often internal than external. To quote the over-quoted Pogo, "We have met the enemy and he is us."

Every day, in sanctuaries across this country, the lifeblood of the gospel is being drained by clergy whose overwhelming desire to be admired and affirmed robs them of their call to be authentic. What gets in the way is the ego, and I say this with some trepidation, since I am a minister with an ego, and rumor has it with a fairly well-developed sense of self. If this is true, then perhaps it is an advantage in disguise, since I'm guessing that all of us who have achieved some measure of success in the world are burdened by the illusion that we are something special.

After all, it is a fact that both teaching and preaching are frequently described as "audacious" activities where mere mortals presume to be wise enough, but also humble enough, to enlighten our students or to mediate the transcendent power of God. The potential here for what psychologists call "transference" is frightening. Yet all of us would do well to remember that whether we are teaching or preaching, we are

not performing. Or at the very least, we perform only in service
to *evocation* in the Socratic sense. Our objective is not to
impress, but to draw forth the truth that lies slumbering in all
of us. We should not be asking at the end of our lecture or
sermon, "How did I do?" Rather, we should ask, "Did anything
happen?" Paul Tillich reminded us that we cease to be
self-centered only by becoming a centered self.

A faculty colleague of mine at Oklahoma City University
taught us this lesson in a most unforgettable way. She was a
gifted professor of English who was diagnosed with Lou Gehrig's
disease. In just a few months' time, she could no longer speak.
What does it mean to be a teacher, she asked herself, *who cannot
speak?* With the help of technology that allowed students to
submit questions on a screen and receive answers from a now
mute professor, she taught her favorite American literature
survey class without speaking a single word for the entire
semester.

What she learned from that experience she chronicled in
a beautiful essay entitled "Teaching with Silence." Before she
lost the ability to speak, she wrote, "I did not fully realize the
extent to which I associated teaching with performance. I saw
the classroom as a stage, with myself, as teacher, positioned
front and center—in the spotlight . . . my teaching self was a
performing self. And my performance medium was the spoken
word. . . . But when I could not long speak, that performing
self-disintegrated. . . . I became a different kind of teacher than
I had ever been. I became a teacher who actively listened."

> Most teachers listen, of course. Back when I still
> had the ability to speak, I prided myself on being
> an exceptionally good listener. Truth be told, how-
> ever, perhaps I did not listen as much as I could

have—or as much as I should have. Truth be told, perhaps most teachers don't. I learned, in my semester of active listening, that I had in the past often confused *listening* with waiting for my students to stop talking so that I might resume the very important business of performing. I learned that active listening can be a nurturing, catalyzing force within a classroom—and I learned that active listening is hard work. I learned that if I listened carefully, thoughtfully, generously, and non-judgmentally, my students would delight me with the complexity of their thinking, the depth of their insight, the delicious wickedness of their humor, and with their compassion, their wisdom, and their honesty. I learned that, in the presence of a teacher who is an active listener—a teacher who removes herself from the center of the stage—students can blossom in beautiful ways.[6]

What would it take for the clergy, or for anyone who teaches, to remove him- or herself from the center of the stage so fully that the truth itself might blossom? Would it not first require that we get ourselves out of our own way, allowing something to come *through* us that can be appropriated, not just heard? Fred Craddock put it this way: "Our job is not to tell people what they 'need to hear,' but rather to get heard what it is that people need to say." How ironic, said Kierkegaard, is "the case of the preacher of repentance who, when he wants to chastise the vices of the age, is much concerned about what the age thinks of him."[7]

Alas, in this high-tech culture we are being pushed in exactly the opposite direction. Ours is the age of the celebrity cleric, dressed down but hip as he paces the stage of an auditorium wearing a button-down shirt, not tucked in, rolled-up sleeves, and black Converse tennis shoes. He has a flesh-colored rock-star microphone draped over his ear and is surrounded by high-tech visuals and thumping music. Many in the crowd grip Starbucks coffee cups with their own names written on them.

Churches are working very hard these days to market their message to a younger, more visual, less patient crowd—even when the results can make it hard to tell the difference between a worship service and a TED Talk. Yet if the timeless intention of true religion is to turn us from selfish to selfless, then consider the irony of living in the age of the "selfie," where people take their own portraits with their own cell phones and then post them on their own electronic bulletin boards of self-aggrandizement. Here is the self in the act of recording the self, packaging the self, and then posting the self online to compete in a worldwide marketplace of other packaged and posted selves. Not so long ago, if you took the picture, you were not in the picture. Now we are all both subject and object.

Teachers and preachers, on the other hand, are supposed to become "superfluous." They are supposed to "disappear" in service to learning. How ironic that we so often hire the most attractive teachers, when Socrates was ugly, "with clumsy feet and growths on his forehead, a condition that Socrates regarded as favorable to his work as a teacher, keeping the students engaged with the subject matter rather than with him."[8]

Grace Can Only Fill Empty Space

To put this in the language of the poem, it is not enough when one idea simply replaces another idea—as if learning is about writing over the top of ignorance to automatically delete

it. First we must fall off our horse, be "involuntarily dismount-
ed," as we say in Oklahoma, from our myriad illusions. And if
we are indeed saved by grace (and the Lutheran in me believes
that we are), it is important to remember that grace can only
fill empty space—meaning those who are always full remain
perpetually empty.

We might as well hang a NO VACANCY sign on our hearts.
Nothing can move into a room that is already fully occupied,
which is why idolatry is at the top of the list of the Ten Commandments. It is the mother and father of all sins. Something
else is taking up all the space that we are supposed to keep "hol-
lowed" out for God. It is why there was "no room in the inn";
why the rich, young ruler "went away sorrowing"; why Nicodemus just didn't get it. For this reason Jesus pronounces a
blessing on those who hunger and thirst after righteousness—
they will be filled because they have available space. Why else
would Jesus teach us in parables, disorienting us before reori-
enting us, when he could have just handed out small tracts to
the crowd that listed clear instructions about how to get into
heaven ("Should you die tonight"), by climbing up each of the
eight rungs on the ladder of glory?

Kierkegaard was happy to think that after one of his discourses, the reader would not remember a word he wrote but
would be left instead with a feeling of having been dangled over
the vortex of truth itself, and to exclaim, "I am undone!" He
would sometimes interrupt his discourses to say this, and then
go right back to his previous train of thought. I don't hear many
sermons or attend many lectures in which I can honestly say
that I feel dangled over anything.

What is redemptive for me is the clarity that comes from
doing the gospel. Wisdom and true enlightenment are the
by-products of action, not of discussions about the need to act.

Feeding the homeless creates a more consistent "thin place" than any white paper on the "problems of the homeless." This spring a seventy-nine-year-old woman in my congregation chained herself to earth-moving equipment near Oklahoma City to protest the building of the Keystone XL pipeline. They cut her loose, put her in jail, and asked her why she did it. "The earth is the Lord's and the fullness thereof," she said, quoting the Psalms, "and besides," she continued, "haven't we talked about it enough?"

The church keeps trying to repair itself by remodeling—doctrinally, aesthetically, or programmatically—but it seems to have forgotten how to resist. In addition to all the duties of ministry (which include the pastoral as well as the prophetic), we are called to embody resistance to all that is false. We are called to resist with mind, soul, and body all that masquerades as truth. We must push back against the seductions and mythologies of the marketplace, the cruel panacea of take-this-pill medicine, and the bankrupt Wall Street bargain that places private ambition over intimacy and stock portfolios over people.

So our first act of resistance is to repent of our illusions—to turn around. Then we can practice resistance as the body of Christ in three critical areas: the personal (ego), the theological (orthodoxy), and the cultural (empire). We begin with the ego because nothing redemptive can happen until we are uncoupled from this monster. Until we stop worrying about what people think of us as "performers" of ministry, and become more attuned instead to our role as mediators of transcendence. Although it may strike some as a biblical cliché, perhaps we really do "find [our] life by losing it," especially in the doing of those non-public acts of ministry that release the real power of what we do—sometimes even to an extent that frightens us.

When leaving a hospital room, for example, or a counseling session, or a trip to a nursing home. Or when called at the eleventh hour to the halls of that groaning and gasping place we call hospice, where morphine is God's gift to dying people. This is when you know something about the power of what it has been given to a pastor to do. Whether you are clergy or not, visiting a nursing home is one of the most countercultural activities on earth.

I'll never forget a visit I made once to what is euphemistically called the "Memory Unit." I had not met the man I was going to see, so I began to look for names on the wall, hoping that I would find the right room. I stuck my head into what I thought was the right room and inquired, "Are you Robert?" A voice came back from the shadows, a plaintive voice from a lump in the bed. The voice said, "I am if you want me to be."

The Irony of the Ego Lecturing on the Ego

British ballet dancer Margot Fonteyn once said, "The most important thing I have learned over the years is the difference between taking one's work seriously and taking one's self seriously. The first is imperative, and the second disastrous." Strangely, in order for the clergy to take our work more seriously, we are going to have to take ourselves less seriously. As my wife puts it: "Get over yourself." Otherwise, how can our lives be "given over" to Something More?

Think for a moment about the irony of someone talking about the ego while giving the Beecher Lectures. You know that you are supposed to be humble about it, but that's not really how you feel. You feel chosen. In fact, once your heart quits racing, you feel proud as a peacock. Then, if you are paying attention, you start to notice the symptoms of a strange

malady that I call PBS, or *Pre-Beecher Syndrome*. Here's how
you know you have it. Once the invitation comes, you begin to
notice strange behaviors in yourself. At first, you may not even
know that you are suffering from PBS. Gradually, however, it
becomes obvious.

Here is the first clue. You will begin to interject into ordinary conversations the fact that you are giving the Beecher
Lectures, even when you are talking to someone who could not
possibly be expected to care. The self-infatuated conversations
sound like this:

> A friend says to you, "Good morning, how are you?"
> You answer, "Just fine. I'm giving the Beecher
> Lectures, you know."

> Or, "Robin, what have you been up to lately?"
> I reply, "Well, thanks for asking—I'm work-
> ing on the Beecher Lectures."
> The person looks confused and says, "Oh, I'm
> sorry."

> A young woman in the checkout line at the super-
> market scans my groceries and says, "That will be
> $34.95." I look at her, confused, and say, "I'm giving
> the Beecher Lectures at Yale."
> She goes right on chewing her gum and says,
> "So is that debit or credit?"
> *How can she not know that it's credit? Extra
> credit!*

Come to think of it, the ego can cause another kind of
affliction, with exactly the same acronym: Post-Beecher Syndrome. This is where you imagine that after you have finished

you will become, somehow, a different person—a member of an elite company of intellectual saints. The fantasy goes something like this: After the last lecture is concluded, there is a standing ovation, and your spouse or partner says, "Honey, that was great!" And you say, "Don't touch me, for I have not yet ascended to the father!"

All of us would do well to remember that whether we teach or preach, or both, *the desire for self-display*, as Phillips Brooks put it, figured prominently in our choice of a career. I am the son of a clergyman, and I was paying attention to my father's life. At some point I thought to myself, "This is not a bad gig." He stands in front of hushed and attentive crowds and talks about love. He interprets the ancient text, and no one dares to challenge him. He breaks the bread and pours the wine at the table of life while wearing a modern version of those broad phylacteries with fringe at the bottom. People joke that he works only one day a week.

Needless to say, it's a powerful thing to want to grow up to be like your father, or to validate his existence and get his approval by doing what he did. But in the case of the ministry, there are dangers as well. First, that you will be doing something to please others, which is a strong need that ministers have. Second, that you will end up playing a role instead of answering a call. The ministry is not like a family business, where old robes and old sermons get passed down to you. It is more like something born in a moment of temporary insanity, when you find yourself in what theologians call a "thin place." That is when the veil between what is and what ought to be gives way, and you feel beckoned by something you cannot name or comprehend. In short, to be called to ministry is to be undone.

There's certainly nothing rational about it. When it comes to compensation, the numbers don't add up in a world where everything has a price. When it comes to lifestyle, the hours don't add up in a world where we are urged to work as little and recreate as much as possible. When it comes to prestige, there used to be more, but these days many of us are embarrassed to tell people what we do for a living, lest we get lumped together with homophobes, climate change deniers, lovers of only unborn children, and those whose contempt for women is breathtaking.

I am on airplanes a lot, and when someone asks me what I do for a living, I sometimes just say that I'm a professor—only because if I tell them I'm a minister they either begin confessing their sins or arguing with me about the existence of God—neither of which makes for a pleasant trip. Or they explain why they don't go to church anymore, as if I must be some kind of traveling truancy officer for Jesus.

But this much I know after a lifetime of being a pastor: the business of parish ministry is not for the faint of heart. Nor is it for someone who can't pass a mirror without checking himself out. I know ministers whose fondest wish is to die in their own arms. Ministry takes chutzpah. It takes gall. It takes an unearthly kind of resolve and commitment. And yet it can be unraveled by self-absorption. Ernest Campbell, the great Presbyterian minister, used to say that there is in the eyes of God no sadder sight than a minister who started out with a calling and ended up with a career.[9]

As American Christianity continues to decline, and many are writing eulogies for organized religion itself, the role of the clergy in the dysfunction of many congregations cannot be ignored. Certain personality types are not suited to parish ministry—and it is the painful but necessary work of the seminary to stop some ordination trains before they leave the station. One study has identified three major personality styles:

the *grandiose*, the *perfectionist*, and the *depressive* personality.[10] All of these, in some way, relate to the ego of the minister. But they also apply to anyone who exercises leadership in a congregation. They call for active resistance.

Grandiose

The *grandiose* personality is easy to identify. Grandiose people simply have no idea that others do not love them as much as they love themselves. They are arrogant and entitled. They suffer from true delusions of grandeur, or narcissistic personality disorder. This is especially prominent in fields where there is a public and performance aspect to the profession. Whereas other personality disorders are associated with *inability* to perform, narcissistic clergy can be huge performers, "because their inflated sense of self-importance drives them on, to show the world just how important they really are."[11]

Other people often feel taken for granted around clergy who have a grandiose personality. The self is so vast that it literally squeezes out the capacity for empathy and thus stunts the capacity to love. One is reminded of Blake's poem "The Clod and the Pebble."

> Love seeketh only Self to please,
> To bind another to its delight,
> Joys in another's loss of ease,
> And builds a Hell in Heaven's despite.

Clergy who suffer from narcissistic personality disorder are preoccupied with fantasies of unlimited success, power, brilliance, beauty, or ideal love. They believe that they are "special" and unique and can only be understood by, or should only associate with, other special or high-status people. They exploit their friends to achieve their own ends, lack empathy, and are often envious of others or believe that others are envious of them.

Image replaces substance, and the minister's public mask "becomes more vivid and dependable than one's actual person."[12] The grandiose cleric often spends a lot of time and money on clerical costumes and is consumed with how things "look" and "come off" in worship. Despite the essential wisdom of the gospel, which proclaims the necessity of escaping from the prison of self, the grandiose cleric actually does the opposite, constructing his own gilded cage. "This is dreadful for parishioners. Their phone calls and questions are considered disruptive and critical. The grandiose minister unconsciously reflects a disdain for detractors. The parishioners will leave an encounter feeling small, incompetent, and insignificant."[13]

Such pastors love to be at the center of attention. They need to be needed, and often exploit the attachment of parishioners that become co-dependent and use passive-aggressive behaviors designed to foster helplessness on the part of the subordinate while reinforcing the power of the clergy. Such pastors love long titles and often travel with an entourage of helpers and supplicants. When speaking at important events, the grandiose minister often provides an introduction of himself that he himself has written. For who else can better describe how wonderful he is?

The joke about a true narcissist goes like this: If he is driving down the street and sees a sign reading "Self-Storage," his first concern is whether it is even possible to fit his self into just one unit. Some years ago I saw a newsletter article written by a United Methodist pastor who had been forced to resign from her church. In saying goodbye to the congregation, she wrote,

"I deeply regret that this congregation has failed to see the beauty of my person."

Perfectionist

The second clergy personality type is the *perfectionist*. He or she brings a kind of hyper-rationalism to the ministry, a can-do, almost obsessive/compulsive pragmatism. Organized around thinking and doing, more than around feeling and sharing, the perfectionist clergy is a great maker of lists. Whether liberal or conservative (the lists are just different), this clergy person leans toward legalism, often moralizes from the pulpit, and is obsessed with the by-laws. In some ways the perfectionist minister is highly effective, given the way the world values quantifiable measures of success, but there is a tendency toward being a workaholic or what is often called a "type A personality." This minister is not good about release time and recreation. He or she feels guilty when not working, constantly checking e-mail while on vacation.

"Perfectionist ministers can talk about feelings and think about feelings, but they go to extreme lengths to avoid feeling their feelings. Anger is the likely exception."[14] This is especially true of righteous indignation, to which perfectionist ministers are highly prone. A perfectionist minister often continues trying to please a parent or parents long into adulthood, and is afflicted with the curse of believing that he or she has never done enough. As soon as something is accomplished, there is hardly time to enjoy it before that nagging question comes, "What have you done for me lately?"

Since congregations will become, over time, an extension of the personality of the lead pastor, those who are led by perfectionist ministers often get the feeling that perfection should be their goal as well. The message they hear is not about how much God loves us, but about how much we should be *doing* for God (which is, of course, never enough). A frequent refrain in such churches is that, "We must be busy, very busy, or we are not doing the Lord's work." That comment is often heard from parishioners who treat other issues in their lives by staying busy, making lists, and keeping a very clean house. As one woman put it, "I just can't walk out the door unless there are vacuum cleaner tracks clearly visible on my carpets."

Such churches can be very busy and yet utterly devoid of grace. What's more, the perfectionist minister is continuously plagued by the intrusions of life as it actually happens, rather than life as we plan it. No matter how organized we try to be, life remains maddeningly mysterious. All our plans are mocked by what can never be planned, so that the day we had all mapped out ends up looking nothing like the day we actually lived. If the grandiose minister needs to "get over himself," the perfectionist minister needs to be "in the moment" and open to what is happening off-script. For example, all ministers will understand exactly what I mean when I say that parishioners have a habit of dying at the most inconvenient times. Or that chaos theory is perhaps best demonstrated in a church committee meeting.

Things fall apart in the church, and must be constantly reassembled—as they do in life, in marriage, in relationships of all kinds—you name it, you are not in control. You are just addicted to the illusion of control. So the perfectionist clergy do a lot of advance planning, developing one-year plans and five-year plans and even ten-year plans. They map out their sermons for twelve months, and then, as my preaching professor put it, one Saturday night the train hits the school bus (or someone shoots and kills twenty children and six teachers in

Newtown, Connecticut), and suddenly you wake up on Sunday morning and nothing makes less sense than the perfect sermon you had planned to preach.

Depressive

When it comes to the last of the three personality types, the *depressive* personality, there may be more ministers who fit this category at one time or another in their career than the first two combined, especially in modern American society. Some of the reasons why so many ministers seem so sad these days have already been mentioned: low pay, long hours, and a diminished level of prestige in the twilight of Christendom. They experience burnout, a depleted sense of self, and a tendency to blame themselves for all the ways in which they have fallen short. But I suspect that one of the major reasons why I meet so many pastors who are depressed is that they cannot negotiate the distance between what they expected to have happen in their congregation as a result of their leadership (at least in the short term) and what has actually happened.

In other words, the same short-term ethos that has corrupted our political discourse, our financial system, and our interpersonal relationships has created a whole generation of ministers who expect good things to happen quickly. The instant gratification culture in which we live seduces the clergy into thinking that in the first few months after their installation they should see increased attendance, new mission initiatives, and rave reviews for preaching, program development, and pastoral care. In reality, most ministers are not fully trusted by the majority of those in their congregation inside of five years. The most productive ministry, in my opinion, begins after ten years and can last another ten years or longer if the minister returns

trust with vision and creativity. But until there is trust, nothing
is possible—*because trust makes everything possible.*

Obviously, I am making a case here for long pastorates.
At Mayflower I will soon complete three decades serving the
same congregation. I am now marrying the children I once
baptized as infants and then baptizing their infants. You cannot
calculate that level of intimacy. Those who were middle-aged
when I began my ministry are dealing with the dark passage
into old age and death, and they have become like adopted
parents to me. Meanwhile, my contemporaries are making the
journey into middle age and soon into old age with my wife
and me. That is, long pastorates give ministers and congregations the chance to grow up together, to grow old together, to
laugh and cry together about all the things we have been
through, about the foolish ways we tried to stay "forever young,"
or made an idol out of money, or tried to raise "perfect" children
who can, and often do, break our hearts.

The depleted sense of self that can afflict so many clergy
whose expectations are unrealistic and whose anger is often
directed at themselves can be a disaster for congregations. They
secretly believe that they are failing at everything, and when
parishioners come for help, they often leave feeling that most
of their time was spent trying to help the minister. "Struggling
with his own neediness, the depressive pastor has difficulty with
emotional boundaries. And church leaders find themselves
feeling drained in their dealings with the pastor. Depressive
attitudes are contagious."[15]

To Be Transformed

All of which brings me back to Anna Kamieńska's
poem. It so eloquently recommends the posture that precedes

transformation. "To *be* transformed," she begins, because this is something that happens *to* us, not something that we engineer.

> to turn yourself inside out like a glove
> to spin like a planet
> to thread yourself through yourself
> so that each day penetrates each night
> so that each word runs to the other side of truth
> so that each verse comes out of itself
> so that each face leaning on a hand
> sweats into the skin of the palm

I wish we read more poetry in church. The poets and the artists almost always see it before we do. They lead to us to the edge of the river to drink, without thinking that they have to pick us up and throw us in. Masters of metaphor, the soul of human communication, they show us what we already know, or what we have never known, or what we think we know but have never fully known by comparing it to something we have forgotten that we know until it is reintroduced to us. Poets light the world on fire. They could care less whether or not we "get it," but instead they lead us out of the shallow end of the pool and into the deep, where we will sink and drown, of course, if we do not stretch out our arms and float.

Each phrase builds upon the one before it in a kind of crescendo of submission. "To turn yourself inside out like a glove"—how does the grandiose personality do that? If image is everything, then what is on the outside must never be confused with what is on the inside. "To spin like a planet"—how does the perfectionist personality do this? It sounds out of control, as if life is not a list after all, or a strategic plan, but rather a kind of wild careering ride through the darkness. "To thread yourself through yourself / so that each day penetrates each night"—how does the depressive personality do this? It sounds like a call to be lost in being itself and to give up linear notions of time, because perhaps our sadness comes from thinking our thoughts are God's thoughts and our ways are God's ways, when in reality they are not—not even on our best days.

What comes next, however, is the clarion call for the ministerial ego to be "undone." "So that each word runs to the other side of truth / so that each verse comes out of itself / and gives off its own light / so that each face leaning on a hand / sweats into the skin of the palm."

I can't know for certain exactly what she means by this, but I hear in those verses a call to *give it up*, to stop thinking that any one of us is any big deal. What's more, that we should stop thinking that what other people think of us is what matters most, or that our reputation among our peers should ever be confused with faithfulness. We are great talkers in the church. We pile up countless words upon people's heads, many of which are dull, familiar, and pale in their theological abstraction. But how many of our words in church these days "run to the other side of truth"? We want to be clever, and we want people to "like" our sermons (the way we "like" things and people on Facebook). We want to be thought of as "well spoken" (like Jesus, I suppose, after his first and apparently only indoor sermon in the synagogue at Nazareth?). But how many of us *trust* the words we are speaking because we trust so deeply the Word from which they come?

"So that each face leaning on a hand / sweats into the skin of the palm." It is almost as if Kamieńska is saying that transformation happens when some part of ourselves, the public part perhaps, the face, *disappears*. "So that this pen / changes into pure silence / I wanted to say into love." Does she wonder why words are even necessary, wishing instead that the pen that wrote them could change into something more holy than words? Or better yet, into love itself? So it is with the audacity of preaching. Silence would be an improvement upon much of what ministers say from the pulpit, and yet we speak because to do so can also be an act of creation, even an act of love, as when the poet of Genesis has God speak the world into being and then pronounce it good. Jesus says, again and again, "You have *heard* it said, but I *say*"— as if his first act of resistance, his undoing, was his refusal to remain silent.

We are not solo performers, after all. We are messengers, carrying what we have inherited and overheard at the table of scripture and translating it into the table talk of our time. But we don't make it up as we go. Our interpretation of the text is not a recreation of the text, but as the poet puts it, "comes out of itself / and gives off its own light." We preach in the hopes that the gospel will be heard, not just that we will be heard. This makes preaching a kind of "twice-told tale"—overhearing to be overheard and mindful that the gospel was once called The Great Offense, for "small is the gate and narrow is the road that leads to life" (Matt. 7:14).

Fear Not

People are quick to remind the clergy and one another that, after all, none of us is Jesus. To which I say "amen," of course. But beware, in saying this (that we're not Jesus), lest it becomes a kind of dismissal from class, a hall pass, an excuse, if you will, for preaching and discipleship that is little more than a report on what Jesus once said minus any holy compulsion to speak your own words in a voice made bolder by his boldness. We can all love a little more recklessly in service to others because he first loved us so recklessly. We can all be a little more urgent in speaking truth to power, given that we wake up every morning on a perishing planet. What will our grandchildren think of us, dozing through the end of the age?

You shall know the truth, and the truth shall make you mad. I live in the city that hydraulic fracturing (or "fracking") built, and we have both new wealth and hundreds of earthquakes to prove it. Oklahoma's most famous troubadour, Woody Guthrie, sang, "This land is your land / This land is my land / From California to the New York island / From the redwood forest to the Gulf Stream waters / This land was made for you and me."

Yet to this day we have lawmakers who believe that this song advocates communism—that the land can't belong to all of us because, the last time anyone checked, most of it belonged to only a few of us. So where are the preachers to say, as independent contractors for the gospel, that if you hate the government, you probably should not be a public servant? Or that Ayn Rand and Jesus are truly strange bedfellows? Why can't we say this? Because we are afraid. Why are we afraid? Because we care too much about what people think of us, and not enough about whether we say what needs to be said at a time like this.

We would do well to remember the words of the late Peter J. Gomes, preacher to the Harvard community:

> Good news to some will almost inevitably be bad news to others. In order that the gospel in the New Testament might be made as palatable as possible to as many people as possible, its rough edges have been shorn off and the radical edge of Jesus' preaching has been replaced by a respectable middle, of

which "niceness" is now God. When Jesus came
preaching, it was to proclaim the end of things as
they are and the breaking in of things that are to be:
the status quo is not to be criticized; it is to be
destroyed.[16]

As for gifted preachers, I like a smooth voice in the pulpit
as much as anyone. But there are times when I would prefer
some gravel, some red-faced stammering, even a little public
anguish from a preacher who has tasted the bread of heaven
and lifted the cup of kindness and now feels a little drunk for
justice. I can appreciate ministers who are considerate and cautious in the way they go about their work, but not when the
house is on fire. I want to listen to someone who knows we are
running out of time, someone unable to withhold the wonderful, dangerous Good/Bad News.

The point of transformation is that *to lead we must first
be led*. No greater illusion hath the minister than the illusion of
his own self-sufficiency, and this is how we begin to resist the
ego as the enemy of ministry. Or, as the poet puts it:

To fall off a horse
to smear your face with dust
to be blinded
to lift yourself
and allow yourself to be led
like blind Saul
to Damascus

So whether you are the grandiose, perfectionist, or depressive type, the ego is enemy number one. It stands between the
repentance we need, the turning around that is required for us

to follow Jesus, and a different kind of blindness. Self-absorption is the root cause of human sin, whereas our orientation toward the other (or *othering*, as we call ministry at Mayflower) is the essence of the gospel. After all, how can you "other" if you are mostly preoccupied with no one *other* than yourself?

Of course, I am not suggesting that ministers, or anyone else in the helping professions for that matter, empty themselves so completely as to become a bundle of quivering flesh up against every human need 24/7. This is the road to a total collapse, a nervous breakdown. Caring for oneself is also important, for as my friend the rabbi put it: "A man who does not love himself wisely and well will make a casualty out of the neighbor sooner or later." Nor am I suggesting that every sermon can be tipped with fire, or that every Sunday can be Pentecost—that would just wear everyone out. There is a place for "ordinary time."

But once in a while, just so we don't forget the cross, I'd like someone out there to think that there is something just a little bit odd, if not dangerous, going on in church. Because if Pentecost was a kind of trans-linguistic miracle of inclusion, with the Holy Spirit acting as interpreter, then how is it that churches have become among the most segregated and mono-linguistic places on earth? What are we doing on Sunday morning now that is tipped with fire, that might set off the smoke alarm, or at least cause a few choir members to wonder if we are buzzed—even at nine o'clock in the morning?

Holding the Camera but Not on Camera

What must be resisted now are not words per se, but empty words, self-centered words, churchy words that sound like someone is reading aloud the minutes of a meeting we all went to—pabulum that passes for Good News, announcements that go on and on and on (between you and me, I think there are too many announcements in church), or group sharing sessions in the sanctuary under the rubric of "joys and concerns" that sometimes cross a line, in my opinion, between worship and public therapy.

All of this can lead to a loss of both movement and passion in worship, and Kierkegaard warned us about the loss of such passion among the clergy. Over time, he said, we can all end up like religious masters of ceremony, ordained hirelings who have long forgotten what it means to be crazy like Jesus was crazy, counting down the days to retirement while protecting the full measure of our pension.

Yet when those who lead the church no longer appear to be on fire for anything, they cultivate congregations that likewise barely smolder. Indeed, many clergy see it as their primary role to put out fires, not to start them. So instead of showing people the way, the truth, and the life—we just show up, "drop the names of famous persons endorsing the product, extol the contributions of Christianity to our civilization, urge attendance to ecclesiastical duties, and occasionally scold the absentees."[17]

For ministers of the gospel this means that resistance to ego is not just a good idea, or a recommended path for becoming more popular and approachable. Rather, it means that an inflated and tender ego is faith's adversary. Otherwise, the desire to be well liked by everyone, or deserving of a raise, or more popular than other ministers, will cause the clergy to withhold information they learned in seminary for fear of offending a generous contributor. It will cause them to avoid conflict with that vocal minority in most churches that constantly test the resolve of those who would lead.

A minister more worried about popularity than about authenticity will edit a sermon on the evils of war because sitting before him are the parents of a recently deployed soldier, and it has become an unchallenged cultural truism that to oppose war means not to support the troops. We are living in a spiritual wasteland of false dichotomies. We do not mean to chip away at the gospel until there is nothing left of it. We never set out to become full-fledged hypocrites. We just get there incrementally—forgetting that the banality of evil is incremental. It is a step-by-step acceptance of what appears acceptable by itself, but ends up taking us to an unacceptable place that we would never have considered going to all at once. What other explanation can there be, for example, to the debate we have been having in this country about whether or not the United States ought to torture people?

This is how a minister becomes largely separated from the life she calls her people to. She reads the text as a paid interpreter, not as someone who wrestles with it, like Jacob and the angel, until she is both wounded and bearing a new name. We still fear admitting that sometimes the text just baffles us, or infuriates us, or even embarrasses us, and so we fail to provide a real model by which the text is fully engaged.

What I am saying is that of all the illusions that compromise the possibility of repentance, it is the ego that most protects our wounded self. It is the ego that whispers to us again and again: *Everything is just fine. You are just fine. Someday the world will truly understand the beauty of your person.* Ironically, what is missing here is *trust*, a word I think we ought to use more often in church instead of the word *faith*. To trust God, to trust each other, even to trust ourselves.

All three of these personality types put us at risk. The grandiose clergy is too hungry for applause to be vulnerable;

the perfectionist clergy so wraps herself in order and the illusion of precision that she appears oddly suspended above the chaos that the rest of us inhabit; the depressive clergy is so perpetually wounded by the shortcomings of those around him that when he tries to preach Good News, what he communicates is "Perpetually Misunderstood News."

It has been said that there is no smaller package in the world than a person who is all wrapped up in himself. So to close, let me share a story about how powerfully we are addicted to the illusion of our separateness. If one of the marks of the spiritual life is to enlarge and enliven the moral imagination—to enter into the lives of others vicariously—then why are so many presumably religious people so blind to what is happening to those around them?

One can only guess that such blindness is nothing new, since when the disciples asked Jesus, "When did we see you hungry, naked, or in prison and fail to feed, clothe, and visit you?" the answer established both a new way of seeing, and an astonishing ethical imperative: the demands of love and mercy are transposable—what is happening to others is happening to me, and your response to the other *is* your response to me.

Falling Off My Horse

I learned how little I knew about the "other" when I was a freshman in college and the Vietnam War was raging. I had yet to be "undone," but in one blessedly painful moment I fell off my horse and was temporarily blinded. I share this story with my students every semester when we are discussing the proper role of the emotions in public speaking.

In a lecture about the power of words to *do* certain things (not just to say certain things), I talk about the simple distinction between denotation and connotation that we all should have learned in middle school. So, for example, the denotative meaning of the word "pregnant" is an adjective, meaning "heavy with young, to have offspring developing in the uterus, to be in a state of gestation lasting approximately nine months in the human female." But when a fourteen-year-old girl says to her mother, "I'm pregnant," there is no denotative effect whatsoever. The mother does not say, "Oh, so you are heavy with young, have an offspring developing in your uterus, are in a state of gestation lasting approximately nine months in the human female." No, she says, "Oh my God!" Most of my students correctly identify this as a mostly connotative response.

When I say the word "Vietnam" in my classroom, I see nothing on the faces of my students. It is just another American war, and they have other wars to worry about now (although not nearly so much now that the draft is gone). But I tell them that if they have in the audience someone my age or older, the word *Vietnam* carries deep and painful connotations. Fifty-eight thousand men of my generation killed, families torn apart, the nation in turmoil—but it doesn't work; it doesn't register, like so much of our preaching.

So I tell them a story, a true story about one night in 1971 when I was a freshman in college and we still had the draft. Back then we had something called the draft lottery—in which a person's birthdate was arbitrarily drawn to determine who would ship out next to Nam (as we called it in those days).

It was a regularly televised event, during which a lovely young woman who worked for the Defense Department would stand next to a large container with small plastic balls inside that each contained a number that corresponded to a calendar date (there were 366 of them, since February 29 was included). She would shuffle the container and then reach in to randomly withdraw numbers to be displayed as birthdates. Suffice it to say that you did *not* want to see your number drawn.

It was not uncommon for young men in those days to have lottery-draft-watching parties. I went to one once, and this is how it worked. Fifteen or twenty of us would gather in someone's dorm room, order pizza, write our birthdates on a blackboard with our names beside them, and then hang it on the wall. Then we would watch, nervously, as the numbers were drawn—hoping that nobody would draw our number.

One night, at one of these surrealistic gatherings, the first number drawn was the birthday of one of my friends. Everyone in the room turned to look him at once, and he turned white as a sheet. Then he moved silently toward the bathroom, went in, and closed the door behind him. No one said a word.

The silence was broken by the sound of him vomiting.

To say the least, the party was over.

At the end of this story, you can hear a pin drop in my classroom (just like you can hear one drop in this room right now). Why? Because now everyone knows, at a visceral and vicarious level, that should you decide to use the word *Vietnam* in a speech (or just in casual conversation in the hallway about "old hippies" or "draft dodgers"), you had better be careful. The ego is the enemy of empathy. That we can live separated from one another is our deadliest illusion. Let us hope that the pain of being "undone" will make it possible for us to undo others.

Words are powerful, powerful things. Let us never be afraid to use them in powerful ways.

2

Undone

Faith as Resistance to Orthodoxy

Christians should give up on "Christianity."

—Peter Rollins

L et us move now into deeper water. It is pleasant sport to joke about the role of the ego in the ministry, or in the academy, or in life itself—but not very dangerous. The narcissist can wreak havoc on any institution, but his dysfunction does not call into question the institution itself. Resisting orthodoxy, on the other hand, will set off the ancient alarms of heresy. Pushing back against the idea that faith is a set of creeds and doctrines demanding the total agreement of "true believers" will conjure the ancient battles that came to define, and then to fatally compromise, the Beloved Community.

If "faith" in the New Testament sense is *pistos* (more verb than noun), then we have a sacred responsibility to remember what that ancient way of being in the world sought to replace, to reconfigure, to redefine. The first followers of Jesus were resisting not just oppressive hierarchies and purity codes, but the very definition of religion itself. The "principalities and the powers" were not limited to the Roman Empire. They included the religious establishment itself, whose legalistic maze brokered access to God and "devoured widow's houses." To be a disciple of the resister from Nazareth is to challenge more than individual sin. It is to resist theological perversions as well.

This can sound seductively exciting, of course, without sounding appropriately dangerous. In fact, I often worry that when a phrase like "resisting the principalities and the powers" rolls off the tongue it may make someone believe that all we need to do is hit the streets, or storm the barricades, or maybe lie down in front of a tank. What I am hoping to communicate, however, is the need for resistance more broadly defined than civil disobedience. Perhaps a better word would be *rebellion*, or, as I have written about elsewhere, that following Jesus ought to be *subversive* again for the cause of love.[1]

Let me be clear about the three forms of resistance being advocated here. Resistance must be *personal*, requiring that ministers resist self-infatuation (ego); that it must be *theological*, as we push back against the idea that Christianity is an orthodox belief system instead of a very unorthodox way of being in the world (orthodoxy); and that it must be *cultural*, as when we push back against the *Pax Americana* (empire) by hiding ourselves, like leaven in the imperial loaf.

The standard definition of resistance is to withstand; oppose; fend off; fight, argue, or work against; refuse to cooperate with, submit to; to keep from yielding to, being affected by, or enjoying. Resistance is not "revolution," to make a distinction that was crucial to Camus, who said we should always be ready to rebel, but wary of joining a revolution, lest we simply exchange one fixed ideology for another.

Such distinctions are not easy to sell, however, in this hyperpolemical age. Everything around us tempts us to sell our souls to a cause, to believe that we are standing with the forces of Light and doing battle against the forces of Darkness. This is true whether you are a fundamentalist Christian who watches Fox News and gets his culture-war marching orders from the Family Research Council or a spiritual-but-not-religious "latte liberal" who practices the pseudo-indignation of the MoveOn.org crowd and often confuses meditation and mindfulness with navelgazing—or the soul with what Ken Wilbur called "the ego in drag."

Resistance is not just about signing on to do battle with some perceived enemy, although the ethos of the warrior and the righteous battle so dominates Western culture that countless Christians today are urged to "stand with God" on every issue (God's position being conveniently identical to their own), and then to do battle with the infidels on the other side in a world of good guys and evildoers. Anne Lamott reminds us that "you can safely assume you've created God in your own image when it turns out that God hates all the same people you do."[2]

The church today is saturated with the language of righteous warfare, calling Christians to "put on the whole armor of God" and circle the wagons against a culture that we are told wishes to destroy Christianity by persecuting and marginalizing its true practitioners. The "enemy" includes those who insist on the separation of church and state, who undermine the traditional family by advocating for gay rights, who defend giving women reproductive choices, and who insist that the best way to take the Bible seriously is not to take it literally.

The operative premise here, however, is that we *know* what true Christianity is, that we are defending something we truly understand, and that an unspoken consensus exists about the true and fixed meaning of the faith. The greatest illusion of all, however, is the idea that anything resembling early Christian discipleship would be recognized, or tolerated, in the present age.

Resisting the Illusion, Not the "Enemy"

The resistance I have in mind is not about a perceived enemy on the left or the right. It goes deeper than arguments about gay marriage and abortion. It is more complicated, more personal, and considerably more dangerous than our endless debates over correct doctrine or worship. But just as our illusions about the dysfunctions of the ego must first be undone, certain illusions about the meaning of faith itself must be shattered. They must be unraveled, swept aside like those spiderwebs that often appear overnight to drape your doorway—the ones you do not see, but into which you walk unaware and suddenly feel clinging to your face. Everyone who walks into a spiderweb tries frantically to pull it off. Illusions are like that. They cling to us.

Again, the most helpful image has already been given to us. We all need to fall off our horse. We need to be made vulnerable by some existential crisis that drops the proverbial floor out from underneath our illusions about what it means to be faithful so that, once again, we are not deluded into thinking that a fiery sermon about the need to resist will do the trick. Or a great lecture on resistance (delivered with or without notes). Or, in the academy, a splendid paper on the history and merits of resistance (published by a prestigious refereed journal). There is value to all of this, but none of it should be confused with the kind of *embodied noncompliance* that I have in mind as a key to the renewal of the church.

Another way to understand the dilemma we face is to consider the perennial confusion between concept and capacity. This was Kierkegaard's obsession, and it lies at the heart of what it means to be "undone." One becomes gracious not by reading a good book on grace, but by acting graciously. I began by talking about resistance to ego because I believe that self-absorption is the anti-gospel. Erich Fromm said, "The real opposition is that between the ego-bound man, whose existence is structured by the principal of having, and the free man, who has overcome his egocentricity." C. S. Lewis said, "If a man thinks he is not conceited, he is very conceited indeed." And the great poet Rainer Maria Rilke said it best: "Make your ego porous."

We should not be "performing" in worship, however much people seem to want to applaud in church these days. And we are not a "brand" in the world of what's hot and what's not, playing the part of the prophet in a largely self-infatuated drama. "Me, myself, and I" is the new American Trinity, and this applies to orthodoxy as well. Our obsession with right worship and right belief may sound noble. It might even be mistaken for deep faith, but it is ultimately a form of individual and institutional narcissism. It promises an end to uncertainty, ambiguity, even mystery. But doubt is a precondition of faith, not its antithesis.

Strange as it sounds, certainty is often equated with strong faith in our culture. We use the word *faith* to describe an unwavering, unquestioned allegiance to some doctrinal proposition. But certainty is not the flag of faith. Certainty is a symptom of faith's demise. Certainty eliminates the need for faith by replacing it with absoluteness. Churches will often advertise themselves as being in possession of the "answers," but they are profoundly intolerant of certain questions. They promise a place to get "right with God," but that may only mean a place to sign on to a set of particular theological claims that will serve to keep the doubts of a "believer" at bay. Doubt is still widely believed to be both a sign of wavering faith and the enemy of truth.

Abraham Joshua Heschel understood doubt to be neither the enemy of faith, nor the root of knowledge. Faith was instead born of wonder, or "radical amazement." So many religious leaders fear doubt because it would threaten to undo by human reasoning that which has been divinely revealed. They argue that it is arrogant to believe that human reasoning alone can be brought to bear on that which is immutable, and thus trans-rational. But doubt cannot disassemble anything that human reason has not previously assembled, so it is healthy, not dangerous. Heschel writes:

> Doubt comes in the wake of knowledge as a state of vacillation between two contrary or contradictory views, as a state in which a belief we had embraced begins to totter. It challenges the mind's accounts about reality and calls for an examination and verification of that which is deposited in the mind. In other words, the business of doubt is one of auditing the mind's accounts about reality rather than a concern with reality itself; it deals with the content of perception rather than with perception itself.... Doubt, then, is an interdepartmental activity of the mind.[3]

Oddly, our paranoia about doubt is based on our misappropriation of the life of faith. This is what happens when a way of life becomes a list of claims about what authenticates that way of life. Inevitably, when theological explanations of Jesus become more important than an *experience* of Jesus, when a closed system has essentially replaced a spiritual encounter, when propositions about the meaning of love are substituted for the embrace of love itself, the church becomes an ecclesiastical house of cards. Those who would blow it down, we fear, are the doubters. But ironically, it may be the Absolutists who destroy faith. They huff and puff, pouring all their energy into defending the scaffolding that has come to replace the body itself. Arguing about the true nature of the divinity of Jesus has gotten a lot of people killed over the centuries. But it has not made a single disciple.

Once beliefs about Jesus have replaced the Jesus Ethic, we turn into a noisy, quarreling collection of fuming, red-faced, self-absorbed guardians of what some have judged to be infallible. The first casualty of this addiction to "sound doctrine" is the time, energy, and money it takes away from mission. When mission work is gone, church people just look like any other special interest group, raising money to engage in self-promotion. In fact, many Christians today appear to be absolutely indistinguishable from anyone else walking the streets—except that they are angry, nostalgic, fearful, and quick to judge what they don't understand.

Many churches in my part of the world (referred to as "flyover space") have lost any hint of being countercultural. They look and feel like the mall, with food courts, coffee shops, even Christian aerobics (whatever that is). The pastor is like a trained vendor, dispensing both a theological product and the incentive to buy. Parishioners are "customers" or "clients" whose shopping carts must contain the right items at checkout time. It has become harder and harder to distinguish between some churches and a game show. What's more, people have begun to tune out.

Although an embrace of the dominant culture by the church-growth crowd seems to have worked well in the short run, now almost everybody is losing members. The church is now contracting across multiple traditions—cultural, economic, racial, political, and theological. Now the "nones" (those who check "none of the above" on surveys about religious affiliation) would compose the world's third largest religion if combined with atheists and agnostics.

Still the argument is made that lack of orthodoxy is the culprit, and we could save "the faith" by returning to the "faith of our fathers" (or mothers). But the truth may be much more disturbing. Namely, that in clinging to orthodoxy and the cosmology it requires, we are forcing intelligent and honest people to walk away. Not only do they not believe what they are being asked to believe, the actual behavior of those who insist they believe it often contradicts the claim that "believing it" is transformative. Put more simply, what is killing the church is the behavior of church people.

God Is Dead, or Just the Church?

The sad (but to me strangely exciting) truth is that the church many of us grew up in is vanishing right before our eyes. Phyllis Tickle borrowed a metaphor from Anglican bishop Mark Dyer, who "famously observes from time to time that the only way to understand what is currently happening to us as twenty-first-century Christians in North America is first to understand that about every five hundred years the Church feels compelled to hold a giant rummage sale."[4] We are all going through the theological attic, trying to decide how much of our doctrinal stuff is still valuable and what should be taken to the curb and sold to strangers.

I love this metaphor so much (reformation as rummage sale) that I cannot help extending it in my mind. So I begin to wonder, for example, how would the church go about putting prices on some of those doctrines? Is there guilt involved when, say, you cut the price of the Virgin Birth in half? When you mark down the Immaculate Conception to make it an "inconceivable" bargain? Or maybe when you decide to just give away the Blood Atonement for free to anyone who will take it?

What about the Trinity? Should we have an auction for each of the three persons—and should it be three-for-the-price-of-one or one-for-the-price-of-three? You can't break up that set. Those pieces cannot be sold separately, and we have the Eastern Orthodox Church to prove it!

I know this sounds a little twisted, but I am a little twisted—having been a parish minister in Oklahoma for thirty years. Last Easter a mega-church preacher had a raffle on Easter and gave away a new car in the sanctuary after drawing the winning ticket out of the baptismal font. I am trying to imagine how that went, exactly—that is, how it "flowed," liturgically speaking. Perhaps it sounded something like this: "And they went out and fled from the tomb, for terror and amazement had seized them; and they said nothing to any one, for they were afraid" (Mk. 16:8). "And now for the moment you've all been waiting for!"

That's good marketing, they say—a church with the Good News and Lucky News all rolled into one, which might be a parable of the church in our time. When asked about the appropriateness of such a contest on Easter, the pastor replied, "I don't mind bribing people if it means I can bring them to Jesus."

My hope in sharing this is to explain why I have come slowly unglued about the church to which I have given my life.

It seems almost breathtaking at times in its parochial theological peevishness. It seemed addicted to winning the dog-
matic lottery, certain that the winning combination can be
found among a plethora of theological formulae. We ask only
what Christians *believe*, but almost never do we ask what they
do. We can recite creeds, but most of us seem blithely unac-
quainted with the singularity of a Christian ethic. "By your
fruits you shall know them" refers not to verdicts but to virtues.
Jesus recruited disciples, not debaters.

In all my work there is a subtext, a conviction about what
afflicts the church and has dragged it down into a state of almost
complete irrelevancy: *People no longer feel obligated to attend
services on Sunday morning pretending to believe things they know
are not true in order to get rewards they doubt are even available.*

Oddly enough, dwindling church attendance itself is an
act of resistance by human beings who suspect that, down deep,
they have been lied to by an institution that often refuses to let
them grow up, intellectually or spiritually. Many have now
learned through their own study (often of books that their
pastor recommended they not read) that both the message and
the purpose of the church today bears almost no resemblance
to those underground Beloved Communities that were first
called "The Way" and were such defiant, anti-imperial, countercultural thorns in the flesh of the Roman Empire.

So if the ego not properly channeled is the greatest personal impediment to ministry, what is the greatest threat to the
institution itself? *What is the greatest misconception in the public mind about the true nature of faith and what it means to be a
Christian?* This question is often asked in the safe confines of
the academy, but not on the street, where the people to whom
we minister seldom feel comfortable discussing such things. If
you ask almost any American, "What does it mean to be a

Christian?" he or she will begin by listing a set of propositions, claims, creeds, and doctrines that demand a choice, a decision—either to be "believed" or "not believed." This intellectual assent to theological formulae is what defines a Christian. Indeed, the British synonym for a Christian is a "believer."

This is the language of the common man. Faith development is spoken about as if it is binary. "Once I was a believer, but now I'm not." Or it is assumed to be a commodity. "Once I had faith, but now I have lost it." Yet it would be wise to remember that these "beliefs" are primarily, though not exclusively, claims about Jesus of Nazareth. They are primarily metaphysical claims that constitute reasons why we should worship him, as opposed to warnings about what might happen if we actually followed him. They are also primarily claims made *about* him by others, not claims that he is reported to have made about himself. They are primarily supernatural claims, meant to justify "believing" in him because he is fundamentally *not* like you and me (thank goodness), rather than claims about how his teachings, if taken seriously (meaning if practiced and not just recommended), could make teachers, healers, and mystics out of all of us.

Thus the fundamental illusion from which we must be disentangled, or "undone," is that the proper definition of the life of faith itself is first and foremost a belief system with behavioral consequences, rather than a way of being in the world whose behavior consequences make clear the things we believe. In other words, *we are not acting upon beliefs so much as we are believing through action*—we are not believers who act but actors who believe. Our love is not the consequence of our having "signed on" to sound doctrine, but rather constitutes its own sign that the practice of unconditional love trumps the soundest of doctrines.

Utterly Ordinary Revelations

For help in falling off our theological horse, we turn again
to the poetry of Anna Kamieńska. This poem is called "Small
Things."

It usually starts taking shape
from one word
reveals itself in one smile
sometimes in the blue glint of eyeglasses
in a trampled daisy
in a splash of light on a path
in quivering carrot leaves
in a bunch of parsley
It comes from laundry hung on a balcony
from hands thrust into dough
It seeps through closed eyelids
as through the prison wall of things of objects
of faces of landscapes
It's when you slice bread
When you pour out some tea
It comes from a broom from a shopping bag
from peeling potatoes
from a drop of blood from the prick of a needle
when making panties for a child
or sewing a button on a husband's burial shirt
It comes out of toil out of care
out of immense fatigue in the evening
out of a tear wiped away
out of a prayer broken off in mid-word by sleep

It's not from the grand
but from every tiny thing

that it grows enormous
as if Someone was building Eternity
as a swallow its nest
out of clumps of moments[5]

After hearing such remarkable verse, the most appropriate response would be silence. Unfortunately, the mainline church is not good at silence, nor do most of us know when or how to break the silence. Even so, this poem makes me think of the sin of orthodoxy, which may be the greatest heresy of all. Fred Craddock taught me that we live our lives *inductively* (from the specific to the general or from the bottom up). Yet out of unexamined habits we often try to teach and preach the gospel *deductively* (from the general to the specific or from the top down). That is, our real lives are made of small things—a trampled daisy, hanging laundry, a slice of bread, a prayer broken off in mid-word by sleep.

Yet how often does the preacher, believing that he or she is the purveyor of the grand truth, not clumps of moments, reverse the lived experience of the listener and start the sermon with those grand truths as if they have been handed down complete from heaven (in an Aristotelian outline, no less). Then he talks to us about eternity by bringing the swallow's nest into the pulpit already built, not "out of clumps of moments" but *in toto* as a self-evident conclusion—as if wisdom comes to anyone with "no assembly required."

In this old model of preaching, listeners are consumers, not participants, left with little to do except marvel at a creed we didn't write, or a cross we have not borne, or a recommendation to travel the road to Damascus without any expectation that we too might fall off our horse. A sermon on the origin and properties of dust is one thing; having one's face covered in it is quite another. Craddock writes:

Everyone lives inductively, not deductively. No farmer deals with the problem of calfhood, only with the
calf. The woman in the kitchen is not occupied with
the culinary arts in general but with a particular
roast or cake. The wood craftsman is hardly able to
discuss intelligently the topic of "chairness," but he is
a master with a chair. We will speak of the sun rising
and setting long after everyone knows better. The
minister says "all men are mortal" and meets drowsy
agreement; he announces that "Mr. Brown's son is
dying" and the church becomes the church.[6]

The rhetorical illusion under which we suffer is that only
in a deductive sermon is the preacher allowed to tell the punch
line ahead of the joke, or start with the conclusion of an argument and then break down the evidence for that conclusion
into its component parts—proving that what you have already
presented as the truth is in fact true. This is what led Kierkegaard
to conclude that the deadliest illusion in Christendom is that
faith is the *transfer of information* sufficient for salvation.

Kierkegaard used the character of the "professor" in his
work constantly, to personify the "tendency to reduce life to
ideas and to translate everything into objective knowledge. [This
'professor'] offers a course in which matters ethical are thor-
oughly treated but in which nothing ethical ever occurs. There
is information," Kierkegaard writes, "but not realization."[7]

That phrase, "there is information but not realization," cap-
tures the fate of so many churches in decline. It is an illusion that
Christianity can even be vital again after its particular, concrete,
and dangerous call to discipleship has been largely replaced by a
set of claims about exactly what God has accomplished in the life,
death, and resurrection of Jesus and "what it all means to *you*."

Indeed, it seems rather remarkable that the church has put so much emphasis on right belief and right worship when so little evidence exists that assent to propositions (theological or liturgical) will alter human behavior at all, except in the most superficial ways. You are "born again"? Congratulations. Can you show me what that looks like? Or to put it rather sarcastically: What has a "Virgin-birther" done for you lately? Perhaps it is simply human nature to prefer ideas about taking action over actually taking action because the former is completely risk free. Or, as one of my seminary professors put it once, "Maybe a lot of people are obsessed with the idea of the Second Coming because deep down they are really disappointed in the first one."

Or, try this question on for size: Is there any reason to believe that once we have prevailed in winning a theological argument we have somehow become a more loving or compassionate human being? Does theological "soundness," as I heard it referred to in my youth, warm the heart, or does it just make us colder and more competitive in our desire to be right? Again, the great gulf is between concept and capacity. The longest journey a person can ever undertake is the trip between head and heart. Christianity's answer is not a better roadmap or a new interpretation. It is the incarnation.

Clumps of Messianic Moments

Our natural response to the "arrival" of Jesus is to think of him "coming down." But the real story is mostly about a "nobody" from Nazareth rising up. It was his concrete particularity, his extraordinary ordinariness, and his mundane lack of prophetic credentials that baffled his followers. He is, after all, just another sibling in the large tribe of Mary and, quite frankly, was thought to be out of his mind. Yet nowhere in the liturgies of the church does anyone ever promise to "be crazy like Jesus was crazy."

What's more, this Galilean sage did not suddenly materialize and begin performing miracles. He did not announce that the purpose of his life was to teach a new way to read and interpret the Torah. Rather, the reign of God would require a new way to live beyond the law. While the Psalmist counsels that we "look up to the hills, whence cometh our help," Jesus seems mostly to be looking down. He begins to methodically turn over every small, ordinary stone on the way—lifting up people as well as objects, dusting them off to reveal no distinction between the sacred and the profane. "For in him, and to him, and through him are all things."

A sign in front of a Lutheran church near my home reads: IT'S ALL ABOUT JESUS. Really? If that's true, and we are called to follow him, then our faith must be substantially about resistance. His was an *imitatio Dei*, an imitation of God. He called his disciples to be an *imitatio Yeshua*, an imitation of Jesus. But nowhere in the synoptic gospels do we find a call to *imitatio Theologica*, an imitation of beliefs.

There are, however, abundant examples of his resistance to the idea that faith is bound up with adherence to the law, correctly interpreted. Or that righteousness requires ritual observance of purity laws. Or that faith is ultimately an inheritance reserved for the chosen. Jesus does not come singing a new song so much as he insists that everyone might be allowed to sing along. He specializes in small things. *It's not from the grand / but from every tiny thing / that it grows enormous.*

Just think for a moment about reading the whole of the New Testament through the lens of inductive resistance: Jesus arrives on the stage of human history from a backwater town out of which nothing good can possibly come. That is resistance to pedigree. He makes perhaps the most fateful decision of his life when he wades into the muddy waters of the Jordan River to be baptized by John, resisting with his body the idea that the kingdom cannot possibly come in the form of a man who stands in line with sinners, or who is in need of forgiveness himself (seldom is this the subject of an Advent sermon). This is resistance to purity and perfection.

Jesus pushes back against the idea that to be one of John's disciples, that highly successful "turn or burn" preacher, is to be permanently defined by a God of judgment and vengeance, rather than by a God of unconditional love. His first and ultimately fatal act of resistance was to be baptized, which ought to be our first act of resistance in the church—even if we hope it won't be fatal—so that we *do something* to trap ourselves in rituals of obligation. Instead of approaching baptism as if it would be a nice thing to do "just in case there's something to it," we should consider it a dangerous thing to do. More than a photo opportunity, or the chance to appease family members, we might want to recall the warnings about the risks of discipleship to so-called family values:

> For I have come to set a man against his
> father,
> and a daughter against her mother,
> and a daughter-in-law against
> her mother-in-law;
> and one's foes will be members of one's
> own household. (Matt. 10:35–36)

Just imagine baptism as a real threat to the status quo, sufficient to cause family members to try to talk their loved ones out of it. Instead of showing up with cameras and plans

for a lovely brunch following the "festivities," mothers would
show up with restraining orders against their sons or daughters,
while those receiving baptism might request a police escort.

In today's vernacular, what if we warned people that it is
impossible to "unsubscribe" from your baptism, just as it is
impossible to block or delete the work of the Holy Spirit? Or
what if we tried to make it clear that baptism is risky, existen-
tially dangerous, and should at least carry a kind of warning
label like food products or prescription drugs? At the very least,
we could remind people that for Jesus it was not just dangerous,
but deadly. Just once, I'd like to hear about a parishioner who
came to her minister and said in a panic, "I can't love 'every
single other.' Will you please 'un-baptize' me?"

This Changes Everything

Jesus rises from that muddy water not just cleansed and
forgiven, but God-intoxicated, hearing voices ("You are my
Beloved"), then spends the rest of his brief and tragic life asking
people if they dare to drink from the same cup. It's not the Holy
Grail we are looking for, but the presence of the holy in every
grail. Then he heads straight into the wilderness of real temptations, and says "no" three times: resisting the call to be an economic messiah by turning stones into bread; resisting the call
to peddle cosmic life insurance by becoming a crowd-pleasing
temple jumper; and finally, resisting the power to be made king
of the world, so long as the Devil owns the mineral rights.

It is all an act of resistance, is it not, to the legitimate
temptations of orthodox religious thinking? Because, what's
wrong with feeding hungry people in a starving world? In his
answer we hear the resistance: "One does not live by bread
alone." What's wrong with a little faith-based life insurance in

a dangerous world? But he resists again, saying, "Do not put the Lord your God to the test." What's wrong with being rich and powerful as long as you promise to use that power to do God's work? Listen to the sound of his ultimate defiance: "Worship the Lord your God, and serve only him."

Then he just up and announces the arrival of the Kingdom of Heaven, resisting the idea that it will come one of these days when things are just right and everyone will recognize it—which means never. Then he recruits disciples, mostly working stiffs, resisting the good advice most of us would get from the human resources department to interview them first. He asks for no credentials, but rather asks them for an immediate decision. "Follow me and I will make you fish for people." I am surprised, frankly, that none of them said, "Can we make any money doing that?"

Truth be known, they weren't making much money fishing. The empire issued the permits to fish, lent the money for the boats and the nets, and then taxed the catch, the production, and the transportation of the fish to market. Lost in the story of the call of the disciples is the relocation of Jesus from Nazareth to Capernaum. It may be the most important part of the story. If you are going to take the gospel to the Gentiles, and stand with the 99 percent, what better place than the largest harbor on the lake of Galilee? That is where the working poor served the urban elites, toiling sunup to sundown just to service their debt. So when Jesus walked by and called Simon and Andrew, and then the Zebedee boys (who abandon their father as well as their nets), it may not have been that Jesus was irresistible so much as that those fisherman were broke. If working isn't working out, then why not try wandering?

Then Jesus goes into the synagogue on the Sabbath in Capernaum and resists the idea that only the rabbis can teach with authority, for he taught as one having authority, "but not as the scribes." According to Mark, the first and most unvarnished gospel, he "immediately" (Mark's favorite word) starts healing people—lots of people. So many, in fact, that the crowds become unmanageable. If our preaching is to be even remotely relevant, shouldn't we remember this fact when discussing access to medical care in this country?

We've got all these lovers of Jesus running around, saying they adore him, the healer of the sick, the good physician—but when someone asks those of us who are well to help pay to heal those of us who are sick, so that when we are sick others who are well might help pay to heal us—the crowd turns nasty and someone shouts, "Let 'em die!"

Even in his solitude, Jesus is resisting. When he disappears, usually to pray, his disciples seek him out and complain, "Everyone is searching for you." In response he pushes back by redefining "everyone": "Let us go to the neighboring towns, so that I may proclaim the message there *also;* for that is what I came to do" (Mk. 1:38, emphasis mine). That little word "also" is a bombshell, because with it Jesus resists the most dangerous idea of all—that God has a chosen people, meaning all others are "un-chosen" or "non-chosen." So he goes again and again to the "other side" (Bible code for where the Gentiles are). And notice, if there is a road that might bring him into contact with Samaritans, he takes it, much to the distress of his disciples who wish he would take the path of *least* resistance.

Jesus, the Enemy of Orthodoxy

On and on it goes, this nonstop ministry of *resistance*—to the idea that lepers should never be touched; paralytics should never be called to rise, take up their pallets, and walk; sinners and tax collectors should never be sitting at your table eating with defiled hands. Jesus pushes back against those who would put old wine in new wineskins; against those who claim that there are women one does not talk to or listen to; against the idea that the observance of the Sabbath is more important than those who might need, even on the Sabbath, to be healed or to be fed.

The whole of the New Testament can be read as a drama of resistance to conventional religious wisdom. This might just be considered an academic curiosity, except for the fact that so many churches today fear resistance to conventional religion more than they fear death by irrelevancy. So much so that the illusion before us is pure irony: *we have become a body of believers that resist the resistance that gave birth to us in the first place.* Or to put it another way, just imagine that you were to disclaim the birth pangs of your own mother so as to honor her memory through your forgetfulness.

I can find no moment in the gospels where Jesus *stops* resisting. Even when he appears to be resigned to his fate in the garden of Gethsemane ("not my will but yours be done"), he is still resisting the instinct for self-preservation. Or when he says, "Father forgive them, for they know not what they do," he is still pushing back against what anyone would expect to be a normal response to an unjust sentence carried out by those who work the crucifixion detail.

Jesus even creates resistance to his resistance in the form of those who try again and again to frame him on some Torah technicality. But he keeps slipping away, resisting arrest without taking back a single word. Then he "sets his face" toward Jerusalem (a.k.a. "dead man walking"), and by doing so resists the most powerful impulse of all—to go on living. Does he know how it will end? If so, he knows he will be the victim of state-sponsored resistance (also known as crucifixion). This was

Rome's version of the public service announcement. Let all who pass by gaze upon the bloody and rotting corpse of the latest resister—thus putting on notice anyone who might be thinking about resisting the Irresistible.

Well, if ever a man had it coming to him, it was Jesus—redefining the family as those who do the will of God, not those who are related by blood. A man who resisted even the method by which people learn about God, becoming a teller of parables that confused people looking for comfort and baffled seekers who wanted to be confirmed, not disconfirmed. This is how Jesus "undoes" people, saying, "You have *heard* it said . . . [past tense], but I *say*" [present kingdom tense], the God you think you know you do not know—not even on your best days. Or to put it in the language of the *Tao*, when you think you know, that is when you do not know. But when you know that you do not know, that is when you know.

You know the lamp should be on the lamp stand, not under the bed; you know that when you sow seeds, some will fall on rocky soil, others on good soil. So do what you can, and then wait patiently for what you cannot control. After all, nobody plants a seed and then stands over it and shouts, "Come on now, grow!" A seed carries its future in its own bosom, and so do you, my subversive friends. A little pinch of leaven can corrupt the whole imperial loaf, and the mustard seed can grow into something as impossible to eradicate as love itself.

If you share food instead of hoarding it, you can feed multitudes, so resist—resist the notion of scarcity that steals bread from the poor. Allow yourself to resist the idea that a Syrophoenician woman (or any woman in those days, for that matter) could not possibly have anything to teach Jesus. When your disciples look for a sign, resist giving them one, so they won't confuse miracles with magic.

But please, please don't confuse the discrete acts of resistance by Jesus with the theological superstructure of the church that was founded in his name. This was not his doing. He dealt with small things, with "clumps of moments." Kierkegaard said, "Christianity is not a doctrine but an existential communication."[8]

Those "clumps of moments" were once all that anyone had to glimpse the meaning of the incarnation. The touch of his hand extended to heal, eyes that looked at you as if you were no longer invisible, a face transfigured in prayer on a mountain, little children crowded around him for a blessing, drooling and fussing and pulling on his beard. The disciples were annoyed, saying, we can get rid of them, so that you too can love children like all the rest of us do—in theory. But he resisted.

There is a rich man who cannot part with his stuff, disciples who argue over future seating arrangements in the Jesus administration, a blind beggar who stops a parade by calling out, "Jesus, son of David, have mercy on me!" And the Lord does what? He resists the idea that this is an intrusion by saying, "Call him here."

On Not Trusting Small Things

How did these "clumps of moments" as tiny and as concrete as a trampled daisy, quivering carrot leaves, hands thrust into dough, and a drop of blood from the prick of a needle grow so quickly into something as grand and abstract as the Apostles' Creed, the Holy Trinity, or the Immaculate Conception of Mary? How did the poet's *drop* of blood grow into the blood-soaked hymns of substitutionary atonement—so that a drop becomes a *fountain* "filled with blood drawn from Emmanuel's veins; and sinners plunged beneath that flood lose all their guilty stains"?[9]

How did the widow's mite, two small copper coins worth a penny, turn into cathedrals so ornate and expensive that peasants labored a lifetime in poverty to build them? Now we have "prosperity gospel" preachers who peddle the abomination of faith as a personal enrichment strategy, sometimes referred to as "name it and claim it" or "blab it and grab it"?

The answer, it seems, can be found in the nature of human beings—of you and me. *We can't leave small things well enough alone.* We don't trust them to take us to heaven. We want a tour guide to take us there, preferably one with proper credentials. We want to be driven there in the safety and comfort of a creedal limousine. For millions the idea of faith has become a kind of doctrinal version of MapQuest with a single route already chosen. We ask for directions from the clergy to make certain we don't miss a turn, complete with assurances that often sound like the disembodied voice of Siri on our iPhones.

Notice that Siri never gives up when we make a wrong turn. She says, simply, "recalibrating." Just once I want to her to say, "You can't get there from here." In that same spirit I believe the church must now stop scolding so many of us who have left "for [our] own country by another road." We are not recalibrating. We are *reconstituting.* We will not be going home on the old road. The bridge is out, and there are no plans to rebuild it.

Let me be clear. I am sometimes accused of not thinking that theology is important, but it is not theology per se that I oppose. I think we're doing theology right now. It is the curse of right belief and right worship that masquerades as faithfulness that has choked the spirit of the church since Nicaea. Creeds and doctrines were meant to answer great theological questions but ended up creating a theological monarchy. In the Middle Ages, once the church had spoken to a largely illiterate audience whose mortal souls hung in the balance, what peasant farmer would dare to ask a follow-up question? The creeds were handed down as divine verdicts from God's own court, and they were meant to settle things, not, like Jesus, to unsettle them.

> It's not from the grand
> but from every tiny thing
> that it grows enormous
> as if Someone was building Eternity
> as a swallow its nest
> out of clumps of moments

Poets understand that the more intimately one knows some*thing*, the more expansively she knows every*thing*. What is detached and abstract vanishes like morning fog, while what is concrete and particular, what is specific, holds its power forever. Human beings do not respond to "motherhood," but to a particular mother; not to patriotism, but to a particular patriot; not to the divine Logos, preexistent with God, but with that word made flesh. There is Christology, of course—world without end. Better yet, there is a nine-word sermon of a Galilean sage requiring no commentary at all: "Repent, for the kingdom of God is at hand." *At hand*, not in the head—right here, right now, in all its earthly, concrete particularity.

Victorian poet Dante Gabriel Rossetti wrote about this once in a poem called "The Woodspurge." Stricken with grief, the poet describes a scene of deep sadness, sitting alone with his head between his knees, staring at the ground. His mind is on his sorrow, but his eyes are near the ground and fixed on some ten weeds, *Among those few, out of the sun, / The woodspurge flower'd, three cups in one.*

The poet's sorrow passed, but not what he saw. The last stanza reminds us of the enduring power of small things:

From perfect grief there need not be
Wisdom or even memory:
One thing then learnt remains to me,—
The woodspurge has a cup of three.[10]

Put differently, the mind is like a gallery hung with images, not with abstractions. "Images are replaced not by concepts
but by other images, and that quiet slowly. Long after a man's
head has consented to the preacher's idea, the old images may
still hang in the heart.... It is true that there are tongues in
trees and sermons in stones but only he who deals with trees
as trees and stones as stones gets the message."[11]

Who Do People Say That I Am?

Once upon a time, Jesus asked his disciples a simple question: "Who do people say that I am?" The answer that came
back was hardly clear: Some say a prophet, perhaps Elijah or
John the Baptist come back to earth. "But," he pressed them
further, "Who *do you* say that I am?" (Matt. 16:13–15).

The church has struggled for the better part of two mil-
lennia to answer that question, but it is hard to imagine that in
response to the original query anyone would have answered like
this: "Some say Elijah, some say John, but the Children of the
Light say, 'the second Person of the Holy Trinity.' " It is remarkable to me that for all our talk about the primacy of scripture,
we are so blindly invested in post-biblical claims. It reminds
me of Craddock's response to a question put to him about the
Trinity, and what he thought about it. "I don't think about it
much," he said. "I'm more of a Bible person myself."

However well-intentioned our efforts to turn the paradox
of the incarnation—that earthly, God-intoxicated particularity—

into a set of theological propositions, we set the stage for two heresies: (1) *intellectual dishonesty* (since in saying "fully human and fully divine" we are really asking people to simultaneously accept as a condition of faith two utterly different categories of being, not to mention a self-contradicting definition of the word "fully"); and (2) the *unintended consequences* of preaching monotheism but appearing to embrace polytheism, or at least Triunism (which is not a word but should be)—and thus puzzling and alienating both Jews and Muslims.

If you are one of those "Bible people" that Craddock speaks of, then you are in for a maddening set of internal contradictions. As Philip Jenkins puts it in his engaging book, *The Jesus Wars: How Four Patriarchs, Three Queens, and Two Emperors Decided What Christians Would Believe for the Next 1,500 Years:*

> The Bible is anything but clear on the relationship between Christ's human and divine natures, and arguably, it is just *not* possible to reconcile its various statements on this matter. In the New Testament, Jesus says quite explicitly that he is identical with God: "I and the Father are one," he declares. "Anyone who has seen me has seen the Father. . . . You are from below [he tells a crowd]; I am from above; you are of this world; I am not of this world." He goes on, "Before Abraham was, I am." His listeners are appalled, and not just because this seems to be an outrageous boast of extreme old age. The words Jesus uses for "I am"—in Greek, *ego eimi*— recall the declaration that God made to Moses from the burning bush. We might as well translate it as I AM. Jesus appears to be saying that he is the same eternal God who brought Israel out of Egypt,

not to mention creating the world. Not surprisingly, the crowd tries to stone him for blasphemy.[12]

In other parts of the gospel, however, Jesus is reported to have made statements that indicate that he and the Father are not "one." "The Father is greater than I," he says. When predicting the end of the world, "he admits that the exact timing is unknown either to the Son or to the angels, and only the Father knows precisely. So if the Son knows less than the Father, the two must be different."[13]

Not surprisingly, it is in John's gospel that Jesus sounds most like a self-declarative, Gnostic contrarian. You know John the Baptist (I'm not John); you know Nicodemus (he is a little confused about being born from above); listen to my conversation with a Samaritan woman with many husbands about the difference between well water and living water (I'll give you water and bread from heaven and you will never hunger or thirst again). And get this: "The one who comes from above is above all; and the one who is of the earth belongs to the earth and speaks about earthly things. . . . He whom God has sent speaks the words of God, for he gives the Spirit without measure. The Father loves the Son and has placed all things in his hands. Whoever believes in the Son has eternal life; whoever disobeys the Son will not see life, but must endure God's wrath" (John 3:31–35).

This is a tad confusing. Is it "Who do you say that I am?" or is it "You had better know who I am"? In the words of the poet, "every tiny thing that it grows enormous" appears to get replaced in John by what others have declared to be enormous and now controls every tiny thing. Perhaps it would be more helpful for the church to read the gospel of John as having occurred in the context of a divorce. Not like the movie *Kramer vs. Kramer*, but the Jesus People versus the Chosen People. Instead of who gets the car or the dog or the place at the Jersey shore, it's who gets God?

We tend to say the most defiant and destructive things as we are walking away from those we love but can no longer live with. No wonder we see this progression in the canonical gospels, from a humble, self-effacing Jesus in Mark, "Why do you call me good? No one is good but God alone" (Mk. 10:18), to the somewhat more assertive: "I am the way, and the truth, and the life. No one comes to the Father except through me" (John 14:6).

John's gospel is written when the Jesus People are about to split from the Chosen People and start living on their own. This makes it a good time to hear someone say what they all needed to hear, that they will be "just fine, thank you very much." You may have Abraham, and all the history that goes with having been the people of God for a long, long time, but we have something even older, the divine Logos, the One who grew up in God's house.

When Does Jesus Become Son of God?

To confront this obvious evolution, from Galilean sage to supernatural savior, is problematic only if we pretend that it is not problematic. At the very least, *pastors have a moral obligation to tell their congregations what they have learned in seminary.* Many do not, unfortunately fearing that to do so would undermine "faith" and cause an erosion of authority (both for those in the pews and for the minister). Ministers talk openly to one another about letting "sleeping dogs lie," but by doing so they are the ones who are lying. We owe it to those listening on Sunday morning to illustrate the changing image of Jesus in the New Testament, not to mention in those radically different portraits, the so-called Gnostic gospels that were labeled heretical and then often hidden.

We tend to think this candid approach will just confuse people. But there are simple ways to make it clear, and then let the people decide. For example, why not ask the congregation a simple question: At what moment does Jesus become Son of God? And why does it keep moving back in time as the chronological distance of the writer from Jesus increases?

For Paul, the writer of the earliest material in the New Testament (early to mid-50s C.E.), Jesus becomes Son of God at the resurrection, when God "adopts" him. For Mark, written a decade or more later (around 70 C.E.), Jesus becomes Son of God when he is standing in the Jordan River being baptized by John. In Matthew and Luke (written in 80 or 90 C.E. or later), Jesus becomes Son of God at his miraculous conception.

Clearly, we keep moving back in time as the author moves forward in time—from resurrection to baptism to conception. And finally, when John writes his gospel (turn of the first century or beginning of the second), when does Jesus become Son of God? He has *always* been the Son of God because he was preexistent with God, the Logos that was in the beginning with God, and all things came into being through him, and "without him not one thing came into being" (John 1:3).

From resurrection to baptism to conception to preexistence—this is no small journey. To point this out to people, as the preacher must, is not to "steal people's faith" by unraveling the authority of scripture. It is to be intellectually honest about the evolving nature of the church's conversation about Jesus, shaped by new challenges in different communities, hardened by conflict and doubt, and forged in the lengthening shadow of the foremost problem in the New Testament: the failure of Jesus to return.

Almost everyone agrees that Jesus was human: he wept, he felt sadness, he lost his temper, and he was frequently exhausted. But the church also made another claim—namely, that this fully human one is also fully divine—and thereby set the stage for the most confounding paradox in the Western world. How are these two distinct natures to be reconciled without the complete sacrifice of logic? How can anything be both fully one thing and also fully something else? Was it God that wept? Had God died on the cross?

Those who claimed that Jesus was fully divine and not human at all could be seen as early as 110 C.E.. With the New Testament still under construction, Ignatius proclaimed Christ as "God come in the flesh" and addressed believers, "whose hearts were kindled in "the blood of God." As Jenkins put it, "God weeping is one thing, but *bleeding?* Even faithful Catholics who accept that the communion wafer is Corpus Christi, the Body of Christ, dare not make the leap that would proclaim it the Body of God. God and Christ are different."[14]

A Man-Bearing God or a God-Bearing Man?

To be honest, I sympathize with the challenge faced by the early church fathers, whose real struggle was to claim the full humanity of Jesus against those who argued for his complete and exclusive divinity. How would Christianity have survived otherwise in an age where so many competing religious systems had supernatural credentials? To put it mildly, however, this set off so many unintended consequences as to give us pause all these centuries later. Was Jesus a man-bearing God or a God-bearing man? Each side found scriptures to prove their point, and the competition was furious and ultimately violent for the prize that is orthodoxy.

Had Jesus been so overwhelmed by Godhood that his human nature was eclipsed and he walked the earth disguised as a man? If so, could he really have been said to suffer, or was it all an illusion? Or was he always just a man overwhelmed by God consciousness that people mistook for God? This may sound like just a fascination with the way theologians once spent their time and energy, but in fact the vast majority of Christians today understand the nature of Jesus based on the findings of the great council at Chalcedon in 451.

It was there that the great debates were settled by divine decree: Christ existed "in two natures, which joined together in one person. Two natures existed, 'without confusion, without change, without division, without separation; the distinction of natures being in no way annulled by the union, but rather the characteristics of each nature being preserved and coming together to form one person.' "[15]

There. That settles it. Except that of course it did not, has not, and will not settle the great question "Who do people say that I am?" Chalcedon's answer was far from the only solution, but it was advanced by political power when the church became its own empire. The greatest critics of Chalcedon were those who stressed a single divine nature for Christ, called the *Monophysites*, from the Greek words for "one nature." They were heirs to some of the oldest churches of the apostolic age. This did not stop each side from persecuting its rivals, however, and in the name of Jesus they slaughtered one another. Tens of thousands of Christians were killed by other Christians to prove that certain knowledge of the true nature of Christ otherwise trumps all his commandments to love one another.

When Edward Gibbon wrote his classic account of the decline and fall of the Roman Empire, he referred to the violence and fanaticism immediately following Chalcedon:

Jerusalem was occupied by an army of [Monophy-
site] monks; in the name of the one incarnate
Nature, they pillaged, they burnt, they murdered;
the sepulcher of Christ was defiled with blood. . . .
On the third day before the festival of Easter, the
[Alexandrian] patriarch was besieged in the cathedral, and murdered in the baptistery. The remains
of his mangled corpse were delivered to the flames,
and his ashes to the wind; and the deed was inspired by the vision of a pretended angel. . . . This
deadly superstition was inflamed, on either side, by
the principle and the practice of retaliation: in the
pursuit of a metaphysical quarrel, many thousands
were slain.[16]

Here is the dark side of religion. Each side had its absolute
truth, and salvation itself hung in the balance. We tend to think
of the Crusades when we think of Christian violence, but the
violence of Christians against other Christians in the fifth and
sixth centuries was greater and more systematic than those
much later atrocities. Fellow followers of Jesus were dragooned
and burned alive, the Eucharist was used as a tool of religious
terror and oppression, and those deemed to be on the wrong
side of the one-nature-versus-two-nature wars, including nuns,
were dragged to the communion table screaming, where the
bread of heaven and the cup of kindness were forced upon
them—because it was believed that once they had partaken,
even against their will, they were now officially in the Chalcedon
camp.

It is a rather humbling exercise to read the work of
scholars on the development of what we still think of today as
orthodoxy. It had much less to do with sound arguments and

much more to do with historical accident and raw chance. "What mattered were the interests and obsessions of rival emperors and queens, the role of competing ecclesiastical princes and their churches, and the empire's military successes or failures against particular barbarian nations."[17]

The Seductions of Certainty

This obsession with being right, with claiming absolute knowledge about the mind of God on such matters as the divinity of Jesus, the authority of the church, the relationship between church and state, the proper way to read and interpret scripture, the ethical conduct demanded of Christians, and the means of salvation, has divided and weakened the church, split families, led to unthinkable violence, and continues to this day to haunt the reputation of all organized religion. It must be resisted. It is a deep wound in the body of Christ as surely as the spear that was thrust into his side.

How ironic that in complete opposition to his prayer in John, "That they may all be one," these schisms led to the collapse of Roman power, to the rise of Islam, and ultimately to the destruction of Christianity through much of Asia and Africa. "History is written by the winners," we are told. This is true of theological history as well. Orthodoxy is both the child of victory and the tool of survival.

Think how far the church has come from the gospel itself: The disciples came to Jesus once complaining that someone was casting out demons in his name but "does not follow with us." The Lord's response: "Do not stop him; for whoever is not against you is for you" (Lk. 9:49–50). In other words, this is not a zero-sum game. It is an *ethic* Jesus was after, not an identity; an *orientation*, not an order.

How much harm has been done, and continues to be done, by people who confuse faith with the possession of absolute truth? Is it not the cardinal sin of believers that so often they are more in love with being right than they are right by being loving? Perhaps this is what must be undone: the illusion that faith is a Grand Proposition instead of a mysterious inclination; a Doctrinal Allegiance instead of an existential capacity; a low-level Mental Surrender to a list of ecclesiastical claims instead of a luminous trust in what Barbara Brown Taylor called the "luminous web." Why else would we fear doubt so much? I recall from seminary days a simple assertion by New Testament scholar Leander Keck: "When the possibility of doubt is gone, the possibility of faith is gone."

How strange that today we insist on theological uniformity within so many communities when those first followers of Jesus disagreed about almost everything: the eleventh-hour Gentiles, circumcision, the role of women, eating meat offered to idols, who is a true apostle, what happens to the dead when Jesus returns (and by the way, why hasn't he?).

These fights are preserved in Acts and in the letters of Paul, but so is something else: namely, that despite those differences, the Beloved Community was subsumed under a single, radical oath—the profession of a transcendent loyalty to The Way—*Jesus Christ is Lord*. This was not a "belief" about Jesus, per se, so much as it was a confession of allegiance and obedience. To his way of being I must be bent; to his order I must submit; to his kingdom I will give my days and die for no other. I will pray *for* Caesar, but not *to* Caesar. I shall render unto him what is due, but that will never include my heart. Just imagine, my friends, the power that the church could exercise in our time if we were not part of the culture's "captive class."

For now, let us consider that perhaps *orthodoxy itself is heretical*. English bishop William Warburton explained the difference between orthodoxy and heresy quite effectively: "Orthodoxy is my doxy; heterodoxy is another man's doxy."

These battles are still with us, of course, in new guises, but the effect is the same. When Christianity is purported to be a belief system with postmortem benefits, the brightest and best among us suffer from what the French philosophers call *La douleur de voir trop clairement* (the pain of seeing too clearly). Slowly but surely, an inherently contradictory message soaks into the bones of those who are trying their best not to give up on organized religion. Here is the best way I know to put it:

Rigid orthodoxy makes it clear that this God of love we say we worship will, in the end, reward a person who believes the right things *about* Jesus, even if he must be forgiven for not practicing the love of Jesus, while that same God of love will punish a person who spends a lifetime loving others *like* Jesus, but cannot be forgiven for believing the wrong things *about* Jesus. It's enough to bring to mind the shortest verse in the Bible: "Jesus wept."

Conformity as Spiritual Plagiarism

When I was in the third grade, I had just started in a new school. Art class was one of my favorites, but I was not very good. In fact, I wondered why some of the other students could draw so much better than I could. One boy in particular seemed to be able to draw anything and make it look exactly like what it was—a horse, a running dog, an old woman's face. His work was proportionate, realistic, disturbingly close to perfect. I hated him.

Our teacher, Mrs. Hansen, wasn't really an art teacher, but she knew good art when she saw it, and she was always praising his work. She hung it up all over the classroom, put it out in the hallway for Parents Night, inside the principal's office, you name it, the message was clear: *this is how you draw if you are a real artist.* We started calling him Rembrandt, or "Remy" for short. We all hated him.

The horses I drew looked deformed; the running dogs I penned had bodies too big for their legs or legs too big for their bodies. As for drawing an old woman's face, the eyes were so-so, but the ears never looked right. And the hands— well, hands are so hard to draw. So I never showed my work to anyone.

One day I approached my friend and said, "Remy, how do you do it?"

"Do what?" he replied.

"Draw. How do you draw so well?"

He looked at me and smiled. Then he reached into his satchel and pulled out what looked like a tablet of drawing paper. But when he opened it I noticed that the sheets were very thin, onion colored, and translucent.

"This is my secret," he said.

"What do you mean?"

"The paper," he said. "It's tracing paper. Watch this."

He took out a single sheet and laid it down on top of a picture of a horse on the cover of a magazine. "See," he said, "the outline of the horse shows right through." Then he took his pencil and traced it, a perfect duplicate of the horse.

"But that's not what you turn into Mrs. Hansen," I said.

"Of course not, you dummy. Watch this." Out of another tablet he took a sheet of regular paper, laid it under the tracing paper, and pressed down hard enough with his pencil to transfer the lines from one to the other. Now the outline of the horse was on regular paper.

"From here on it's easy," he said. "Just add the colors you see on the original and you've got yourself one fine picture of a horse.

"Tracing paper, Robin. That's all you need."

So I got some and tried it! My art definitely improved, but there was something missing. Then one day Mrs. Hansen saw some of my new work and exclaimed, "Oh, Robin, how beautiful! You have made such amazing progress. Would you mind if I hung some of your work up for the others to see?"

"No . . . I mean yes, I do mind . . . I mean no—please don't hang it up!"

Tracing the Faith

So what does this story have to do with faith? Perhaps we've all heard too many sermons that sounded like the preacher put tracing paper over the text and called it "Good News." Traced the outlines of Acts 2 and called it a Pentecost sermon. Read the Beatitudes as if she were reading an ordinary grocery list. Copied the father of the prodigal son as if all disgraced patriarchs would run to meet their whoring lads and embrace them still reeking of cheap perfume and pig shit.

So much in church these days seems "lifted clean" from a page that once ran red with blood. So much preaching is devoid of the urgency of faithful Midrash, lifeless in its sentimental re-gurgitation of the passion of others. Now, thanks to the Internet, the exegesis of the text comes online, a click or two removed from the work of scholars, effective illustrations, and sermon templates ready for a pulpit version of take and bake, no fuss or muss.

Princes of the pulpit post their wares as if marked "Good for any occasion." Edification has replaced risk. Efficiency has replaced terror. A toastmaster's bag of tools has replaced

Abraham's raised knife over the helpless and squirming brown body of his beloved Isaac. Every time the scribes and Pharisees murmur, or mumble, or begin seeking ways to destroy him, the preacher traces those stories with such vapid two-dimensional tonality that nobody listening feels a thing. Droning we are used to in church. Murmuring not so much.

I fear that countless Christians have traced their confessions as if with an imaginary pencil in the air, outlining the contours of someone else's way of solving someone else's problem. Watch my hand now as I trace the Apostles' Creed:

> I believe in God the Father, Almighty, Maker of heaven and earth: And in Jesus Christ, his only begotten Son, our Lord: Who was conceived by the Holy Spirit, born of the Virgin Mary: Suffered under Pontius Pilate; was crucified, dead and buried: He descended into hell: The third day he rose again from the dead: He ascended into heaven, and sits at the right hand of God the Father Almighty: From thence he shall come to judge the quick and the dead: I believe in the Holy Ghost: I believe in the holy catholic church: the communion of saints: The forgiveness of sins: The resurrection of the body: And the life everlasting. Amen.

Time to put down the pencil and take up the poet. Maybe Kamieńska is right when she says that faith does not begin with a grand outline of a medieval drawing of the swallow's nest of salvation, but instead with *small things*, with clumps of messianic moments that we must be bold enough to sketch with the free hand of our hearts . . . *the blue glint of eyeglasses . . . a splash of light on a path . . . a bunch of parsley.*

If we must be orthodox, should we not consider an ethical, rather than a metaphysical orthodoxy? Is not the Sermon on the Mount our true orthodoxy? Could our way of *being* in the world, not our beliefs, be the only creed we carry? Our faith does not begin with propositions and end with assent. It begins with astonishment and ends, by grace, in imitation. We do not look at Jesus and see a God Man, but rather a man so well acquainted with God as to shame what we think it means to be human.

The church can no longer exist as a boys' club, or a heavenly pyramid scheme, or just another version of Rotary with familiar hymns, dripless candles, and lots of theological tracing paper. The poets of this and every age are not calling us to confirmation. They are calling us to worship. They are not calling us to copy, recite, and believe, but to encounter radical amazement in small things—*as if Someone were building Eternity as a swallow its nest out of clumps of moments.*

3

Undone

Faith as Resistance to Empire

Jesus and the movements he catalyzed can be understood only in the context of the Roman imperial order and resistance to it.

—*Richard Horsley*

L et us move now into the deepest water of all. We have been talking about faith as resistance—to ego, to orthodoxy, and now, last but not least, to empire. It is no accident that I saved this topic until the end, since about few things are ministers more anxious, or more prone to hypocrisy, than when we are denouncing the evils of the empire that protects us, enriches us, and gives us special tax breaks.

We know that Jesus resisted the ways of Rome, and that his first followers called him Lord, which meant that Caesar was not. Yet we still suffer under the illusion that *we don't live in an empire.* This illusion is deep and deadly and must be undone.

It is not my purpose here to join the argument about whether America should be referred to using the E-word, which is repugnant to some. They associate it with the *Death Star*, and prefer euphemisms like "great power," "hegemon," "unipolarity," "world leader," etc. It is even repugnant to President Obama, who said recently at the United Nations, "The notion of American Empire may be useful propaganda, but it isn't borne out by America's current policy."[1]

I must respectfully disagree, and suggest that the final proof of empire lies in the extent to which we exercise *imperial influence*—militarily, economically, and culturally. Our methods are not identical to those of Rome, obviously, but the fact is that, according to a recent Pentagon report, "the United States has 662 overseas bases in 38 different countries."[2] By some estimates, we have military personnel in 148 countries.

We wage preemptive war (that is, wars fought to save us from what we think might happen if we don't wage them), including the 2003 invasion of Iraq, to save us from nonexistent weapons of mass destruction. History may record the outcome as having originated in the worst and most duplicitous U.S. foreign policy decision in the modern age. The dominoes were meant to fall toward democracy. Now they are falling toward chaos.

The American empire disposes of leaders who oppose U.S. policies, and we maintain our economic power by guaranteeing our own oil and energy security. We prop up the dictators when we need them, and then destroy them when we don't. We are the world's largest exporter of weapons. We are the world's only superpower, a colossus astride the planet—admired, feared, and deeply resented around the world.

I do agree with those who say we are an empire in decline, but I disagree vehemently with those who say we are not an empire to begin with. Our total military expenditures annually are more than the countries with the ten highest defense budgets combined. We do this in the name of spreading freedom and democracy, of course, and that mantra is repeated in the media ad nauseam when our soldiers are thanked for "defending our freedom"—even when they defend it against those who never actually threatened it in the first place.

One of the distinguishing marks of empire is to hear its leaders speak about the dangers of avoiding a so-called power vacuum. The premise of such a statement is that there must be one dominant power to bring order to the world, without which chaos will ensue. Rome understood its role to rule the Mediterranean world as divinely ordained. Listen to this description and ask yourself if its relevance to America (and all colonial powers) is not painfully obvious?

> Romans saw themselves as a superior people, a "people of Empire." They viewed other peoples as inferior in various ways, needing the domination of a superior people. . . . Rome itself was somehow destined to achieve world supremacy. The torch of civilization had passed from Troy to Rome (see Virgil's *Aeneid*). Rome was favored by the gods; history was moving through its good fortune. . . . The elites of Greek cities built monuments and temples, established games and festivals to honor Augustus/Caesar as the Savior who, under the guidance of divine Providence, had brought Peace and Prosperity to the whole world.[3]

The first followers of Jesus may have understood the kind of "negative peace" that overwhelming force can bring. But peace is more than just the absence of conflict, or the interlude between conflicts (what the Pentagon calls a state of "permanent pre-hostility"). The followers of Jesus had no illusions, however, about the world in which they lived, shaped by Roman power from top to bottom. It was not just the sword, but the empire's elaborate hierarchy that enslaved human beings. Order could be kept not only by client rulers but also by subject-on-subject violence, mutual distrust, and the crippling dependency that poverty creates. Only survival is a stronger force than rebellion. No one bites the hand that feeds until there is an alternative source of food.

To divide and conquer is the credo of empires, so the Jesus People formed spiritual collectives, if you will, underground systems of both material and spiritual self-sufficiency that bypassed the state's patronage system. They could not take up arms against Rome, but they could provide an alternative kingdom that reordered religious life outside the Temple, meeting in clandestine and joyful noncompliance with the principalities and the powers. They lived as BELOVED COMMUNITIES OF DEFIANCE. They emerged as a dissident movement in the Mediterranean world from the bottom up, open to the spirit, animated by faith. It was the era of *shalom*, a reign of God that would include both Jews and Gentiles. "The poor would be vindicated, the outsiders brought within. For nearly three centuries the Age of Faith thrived. Then, however, in a relatively short time, faith in this inclusive new Reign faded, and what had begun as a vigorous popular movement curdled into a top-heavy edifice defined by obligatory beliefs enforced by a hierarchy."[4]

The first Jesus People often met in secret, scratching the sign of the fish on doorposts to mark the spot. Whatever else one might say about modern Christianity, no one describes it as an underground movement. Now we market our location in affluent suburbs with enormous crosses and electronic signs by the highway. Any move by the church today to subvert the dominant culture is met with charges of "socialism" and/or lack of patriotism.

If you read Acts 4, however ("no one claimed private ownership of any property, but all they owned they held in common . . . so there was not a poor person among them"), you might choose a stronger word than "socialism" to describe the early Jesus People. Where did that spirit go? Why is it that no one today thinks of the church as even the least bit dangerous, much less a thorn in the imperial flesh? Isn't it true that we are much closer to what one theologian called the empire's "compliant acolyte"?[5]

So here is my question, plain and simple: *What happened to the church that once gave the empire fits, and now fits right in with the empire?*

Furthermore, is there anything in our time that would more clearly mark off the church as genuinely subversive to the status quo than for us to once again resist the illusions of empire—especially the myth of redemptive violence? The church of Jesus Christ today rides the horse of empire, but we need to be thrown off. We are altogether too comfortable in this saddle of death. Illusions about being a "Christian nation" must also be undone. Evangelicals are correct, in my opinion, when they say that the cross is at the center of our faith, but not as the mark of a cosmic bargain—rather of cosmic *resistance*, the ultimate symbol of the lengths to which love will go to save us from ourselves.

Who Opened the Jesus File?

When I look at a cross, any cross, I see not a piece of jewelry, but rather an icon of Roman brutality—the executioner's misplaced pride in the power of death to have the last word. Rome, like all empires, knew that when you have a problem with some*body* all you have to do is get rid of the body.

"Is he dead?"
Yes.
"Are you sure he's dead?"
Yes, he's dead.
"Put a spear in his side just to make sure. Now pull it back out—there, now he's dead, right?"
Yes, he's dead!
"Good, now put the body in a big tomb, roll a big rock up in front of it, and post a couple of guards there all night. Oh, and be sure to tell them stay awake, or sure enough some*body* will steal the *body* and we'll have a cult of the risen *body* on our hands!"

Empires are in the body removal business. That's how you put down an uprising. You have to make an example out of some*body*. Then you disperse the crowds, hose down the area, make a report, and *close the Jesus File*. It is simple, traumatic, and brutally efficient. Any passerby could gaze upon the rotting corpse, picked over by birds and torn at by wild dogs, and the message would be clear: WHATEVER THIS MAN DID: DON'T DO IT.

To be honest, I suspect that the Jesus File stayed closed for more than the gospels' three metaphorical days. So who opened it? Perhaps scholars like Kathleen Corley, among others, are right when they say that it was women who opened it—women who went to the gravesite to perform funeral rituals, what was called the *Cult of the Dead*. They prepared food, offered lamentations, and called forth the spirit of the deceased. By itself this would not be unusual or unique, but they did this for Jesus in defiance of Roman prohibitions against just such rituals, especially for the victims of crucifixion.

Why was this dangerous? Why was it forbidden? Because to give a proper burial to the victims of execution, and then to have public ceremonies of grieving, was to spoil Rome's intended effect. The empire's message went far beyond "King of the Jews." It was also Rome's way of making a person, and everything he stood for, "disappear." The real message was: BEHOLD A NOBODY WHO HAS COME TO NOTHING AND NOW IS NOWHERE.

One can only imagine that after this gruesome public spectacle, a Roman version of the state worker did his job as a part of the crucifixion detail. Perhaps he wore a first-century version of the reflective vest, boots, and stocking cap. He reported in this case to Golgotha to "do his job." He tries not to get involved on a case-by-case basis. He just manages the crowd, cleans up, and closes the curtain by saying, "You people need to go home now. It's all over."

Yes, of course it is.

Except that it wasn't.

It was the women who resisted first, defying Rome through their graveside vigils. It was the women who brought food, broke bread, and raised the spirit of the Beloved—perhaps even giving us a model for the Eucharist. In the gospels, you may have noticed, women move *toward* the cross; men move *away* from it. Women *do* things. Men *debate* things—often while walking to Emmaus.

My point is that the church was born as an act of collective defiance, and it prospered as a community of resistance. Easter is not just the sound of a solitary bird singing after a violent thunderstorm (as lovely as that metaphor may be). It is the Stone of Hope, covered with nail prints, and rolled away with tears. This is the Easter message: Rome said no. God said yes. And preachers need to thank the women first.

This singular act of cosmic resistance renders foolish, even petty, all our arguments about what "really" happened to the body of Jesus. We are not trading stories about a disappearing and reappearing corpse. We are asking people whether they believe in both the short-term and long-term victory of Love Itself over the empire. Why do we still look for Jesus in the sky when the real miracles are always happening on the ground? Why do we look for a sign from the powerful, when from the beginning it was the most powerless people on earth who conspired to raise Jesus from the dead? How did they do it? They refused to surrender the vision. They refused to forget. They were like leaven that was already hidden in the imperial loaf.

Where Did This Quiet Rebellion Go?

What began as a quiet rebellion of mourners soon grew into a movement that inspired collective, "embodied" noncompliance with the status quo. Vertical and hierarchical religion was "flattened" by a horizontal and democratic egalitarianism. Women could speak and lead. Half-breeds could find a place at the table. To be a "Gentile lover" was not an insult, but the norm. Tribalism was trumped by joy. All the divisions of human contrivance were swept away, or melted down and poured into the Holy Grail of Everybody-is-Somebody at the Open Table. On the outside, all roads might lead to Rome. But on the inside, there was just one straight highway through the desert. The reign of the unclean God of distributive justice had begun.

In just a few centuries, however, it would all start coming apart. The bride of Christ would be wooed and bedded by Constantine at Nicaea. In need of compassionate volunteers to help Rome's poor, and believing that the Christian God had made him lucky in battle, the politically astute Constantine not only paved the way for the church to become the official religion of the empire. He also provided a model by which the church became an empire of its own—all male, top down, take-no-theological-prisoners. Soon the Pope would reign as a kind of ecclesiastical monarch, heaven's appointed one, the Caesar of Jesus.

Although this church/state wedding may have been arranged, there were so many benefits to those in power that I suspect the bishops came dressed for the occasion. It meant the end of persecution and the beginning of imperial largesse. They knew who signed their checks, and we know who signs ours. In American churches, all who give to support the work of the anti-imperial Jesus get a tax deduction from the empire. How nice. The clergy also get a special tax break called a housing allowance.

This is a much-coveted (but unconstitutional) clergy benefit that subsidizes (and thus favors) one class of religious professionals over other citizens. Clergy can exempt from taxation all the money we spend to own and maintain our homes if we do not live in a parsonage. We get this tax break, and then we are allowed to "double dip" (so-called because we can still write off the mortgage interest on the income used to buy a home that we did not have to report as income in the first place). Sounds wonderful, and it has saved me a bundle over the years. Except that like all other special privileges granted by the empire, those on the receiving end lose a measure of their autonomy. It gets much, much harder to bite the imperial hand

that feeds you. Before you know it, there's an American flag in
the sanctuary that you dare not move, and the preacher sounds
more like a chaplain in the pulpit than a prophet.

The Bible Is Not About Religion

In America, the Bible has been used primarily to preserve
the status quo, rather than to challenge or change it. People still
argue over the term "social gospel"—*as if there is any other kind*.
We continue to make distinctions between individual sin and
collective social sin; between private misconduct and public
corruption; between salvation of the soul and salvation of the
system. This separation of private piety from public engagement
has been toxic for the church. It conjures the cartoon of people
praying inside a sanctuary while people outside are starving,
homeless, and persecuted.

As Walter Rauschenbusch put it, "Whoever sets any
bounds for the reconstructive power of the religious life over
the social relations and institutions of men, to that extent denies
the faith of the Master." *It is a myth that the gospel of Jesus Christ
can ever be personally redemptive without being socially responsible.* If there is one distinction that is crucial for the future of
the church it is this: charity and justice are not the same thing.

Our formative story is not a tale of personal piety, but of
daring and sometimes deadly dissent. Resistance is in our DNA.
The spirit is not just a "balm in Gilead." It's a troublemaker—in
Damascus, Denmark, and Denver; in Selma, South Africa, and
Sarajevo; in Philippi, Palestine, and Peoria. The spirit will not leave
us alone. It awakens us to the simple but unbearable fact that the
world as it is cannot possibly be the world that God intended.

And yet, this prophetic sensibility is not like a costume
one can slip in and out of. Should any one of us consider a life

as radical as those Richard Horsley calls "Jesus and other prophets of resistance," then that person is going to be hopelessly
entangled in a dilemma. He or she will be immediately captured
by the fantastic seductions of imperial power, trapped by the
illusion that the empire is morally neutral toward the church.
He or she may even believe that the empire loves the church
and the gospel it proclaims, and will go to war to protect the
right to condemn (and ultimately eliminate) the very foundation on which all empires are built—the assumed premise (most
deadly of all enthymemes)—that *violence is redemptive*, that
peace comes through victory.

It is precisely this "long view" of the church as a force for
redemption—the arc of history that bends toward justice, as
Dr. King put it—which makes it imperative to resist the empire
in the short run, not just to pray for its demise in the long run.
The empire loves anything that delays action "until a more appropriate time." In the meantime, the heart of the gospel and
the heart of the empire constitute the ultimate oxymoron. Peace
through victory is an illusion that must be undone. Victory
does not bring peace, "but only a lull—whether short or long—
and after each lull the violence required for the next victory
escalates."[6]

Put simply, followers of Jesus have always been called
to resist, with heart and soul and mind (and yes, even in a
Pauline sense with our bodies), the very oppressive systems we
live in, work for, are enriched and protected by, and whose
material abundance we conspicuously consume—no easy task.
Just as Moses came against Pharaoh and Jesus came against
Rome, so must the church complete the story by coming against
this, and every empire that displaces the power of love with
the love of power. We cannot do otherwise and call ourselves
faithful.

This is extremely difficult, of course, because the empire operates like a pyramid scheme, as Walter Brueggemann put it. It brainwashes everyone in the neighborhood into believing that everyone can win if they work hard enough. Those on the top are virtuous and favored by God. Those on the bottom are lazy and thus deserve their immobilizing shame. The empire will always define success or failure as entirely *individual* consequences, never as systemic ones. Ours is the age in which more and more people work harder, and longer, and are more productive than ever, but still fall further behind. The American middle class is disappearing, and yet miraculously the workers blame themselves. As Harvey Cox put it, "We don't just live in the Empire. The Empire lives in us."

Empire, or Empires?

Perhaps it would be more accurate to say that the empires (plural) live in us, and that together they form domination systems from which we cannot extricate ourselves without putting everything we are taught to value at risk: comfort, safety, material possessions. These are as attractive to would-be prophets as to the most unrepentant plutocrats. We love our stuff.

For example, just think of the irony, vis-à-vis Kierkegaard, of carrying around our electronic devices of convenience (especially the ubiquitous cell phone) that are manufactured by people whose faces we would rather not see, assembled in places we would rather not visit, and made under conditions Jesus would find appalling. With mock indignation, we create "events" on social networking sites to denounce our loss of privacy, all the while writing on the empire's tablet, thereby dutifully creating data to be mined by those who intend to violate that privacy and then lie about it.

It was Kierkegaard who warned us of the primary danger of illusions, which is that *we are deluded about being deluded in the first place.* It is the nature of illusion, he said, to caress, to free us from the pain that comes from confronting the world as it really is. It is the one who shatters the illusion who brings pain: "Are you able to drink the cup that I am about to drink?" (Matt. 20:22).

So, lest we get ahead of ourselves, we should be clear about what these empires are, which, taken together, form the *Pax Americana.* And what is our definition of empire? Richard Weaver, a great rhetorician who taught at the University of Chicago, once said that a true teacher is a "definer of words, and a defender of their true definitions." So, by empire I do not mean, of course, a kind of apple, similar to a Macintosh, or an adjective to describe the state of New York, or a dress with a high waist, but rather "a political unit having an extensive territory or comprising a number of territories or nations ruled by a single supreme authority."

A secondary definition may be more appropriate for this discussion, however. An empire exerts "imperial or imperialistic sovereignty, domination, or control." We tend to think of empire in strictly military terms, but imperial sovereignty, domination, or control happens in many other ways.

For example, there is an American entertainment and mass media empire that influences much of the world by its fantastic representation of *life as it is not.* Nothing is more unreal today than so-called reality programs. There is an American political empire that pretends to be about the "people's business," while in reality serving only money and power. There is an American cultural and religious empire that rewards conformity and obedience to a dull and doctrinaire model of what it means to be fully human—which is another way of saying that watching television and going to church can have an equally anesthetizing effect. I remember William Sloane Coffin, Jr., talking about the "flatlining" of the American soul, and how it affected even (or especially) the clergy: "Afraid of sorrows too deep we avoid joys too intense, and we call this emotional mediocrity the 'good life.'"

It's true. The empire *flattens* us, packages us, and numbs us through what George Orwell predicted would be a kind of mental opiate delivered through the omnipresent "telescreen." Today, Big Brother is the giant flat screen whose blue light oscillates day and night in almost every American home: the television set, the boob tube, with its commercially sponsored electrons humming day and night with scenes and soundtracks of utter nonsense. Nothing is real; everything is for sale; life is reduced to a commodity in what Kierkegaard called "the sickness unto death."

Just consider, for example, the endless chatter on professional sports talk shows. Grown men sit in studios with sets that look like man-caves for video-gamers, framed by the graphics of Roman Transformers while verbally hyperventilating over trades as if they are talking about the fate of nations. Who will go first in the NBA slave draft (we still buy and sell bodies), and how will it affect Cleveland's future, or Miami's chances, or L.A.'s claim to celebrity fame? Where are the preachers when we need them, to say, "Who really gives a damn about which member of the athletic criminal class gets traded to which owner of the corporate criminal class? Real people in the real world are starving to death."

Screens fill our homes with unreality, stealing precious hours of our lives with mindless programming spectacles built on public humiliation (some participants dance well and sing well, and others get insulted or voted off the island). *Television is the fully automated foot soldier of the empire.* It hangs in the gallery of our minds images of perfection, which none of us will ever achieve, but which afflict the masses with such longing and feelings of unworthiness that we will order that piece of exercise equipment and pay for it later—long after we have stopped using it.

If fact, some scholars would argue that the empire is no longer a nation-state, but *neoliberal capitalism.*[7] Indeed, the rise of the corporation as a class of constitutionally protected persons (*Citizens United v. Federal Election Commission*) suggests that markets drive foreign policy more than borders, and that the religious freedom of the owners should be protected while those of the workers are not (*Burwell v. Hobby Lobby*). If that is true, then how should faith communities resist the illusions and cruelties of "whatever the market will bear"? What new consumer habits would bring us closer to the "socialism" of the early church, and what does it mean that human beings stare at a screen in a mindless stupor for six to eight hours a day? There used to be a bumper sticker out there that said, simply, KILL YOUR TV. I'm beginning to think this might be a Christian imperative.

The Greatest Deception Is the Greatest Illusion

Yet about few things does the empire deceive us more than it deceives us about war. It is both big business and unspeakable horror. By controlling the images we see, by inventing euphemisms that spare us the terrible truth, the empire stunts our empathic imagination. War is outsourced now like everything else. It is a special job done by special people, and we'd rather not see the details, thank you very much. What I am saying here is that the church needs to get its rhetorical "mojo" back and call war exactly what it is from the pulpit: *the closest thing on earth to a state of pure sin.*

John Dominic Crossan speaks of empire as the "brutal normalcy of civilization."[8] He asks two questions that are familiar to all of us. First, he wonders whether this brutal normalcy (by which he means imperial violence) is simply civilization's drug of choice or, second, whether it is the inevitable consequence of human nature.

Whichever is correct (and the Bible itself carries on one long argument from start to finish about whether God is in the business of retributive violence or distributive justice), one simple fact cannot be ignored. Our gospel was birthed in resistance to the "brutal normalcy" of the Roman Empire. The Jesus People, like other resisters before them, co-opted and then reversed the empire's most sacred rhetoric. How do we know this? Crossan put it this way:

> There was a human being in the first century who was called "Divine," "Son of God," "God," and "God from God," whose titles were "Lord," "Redeemer," "Liberator," and "Savior of the World." Who was that person? Most people who know the Western tradition would probably answer . . . Jesus of Nazareth. And most Christians probably think that those titles were originally created and uniquely applied to Christ. But before Jesus ever existed, all those terms belonged to Caesar Augustus. To proclaim them of Jesus the Christ was thereby to deny them of Caesar the Augustus. Christians were not simply using ordinary titles applied to all sort of people at that time, or even extraordinary titles applied to special people in the East. They were

taking the identity of the Roman Emperor and giving it to a Jewish peasant. Either that was a peculiar joke and a very low lampoon, or it was what the Romans called *majestas*, and we call high treason.[9]

So, my friends, let's ask the obvious question: *When was the last time that anything this dangerous happened in the American church?* Does anyone head off to Sunday morning service around here and look in the rearview mirror to see if they are being followed? Do clergy encrypt their sermons as if they were corrupting leaven, to keep them out of the hands of the NSA, or the FBI, or the CIA? Do we pass around our prayers and meditations in dark brown envelopes dropped at secret locations? When was the last time that anyone worried about a sermon showing up on WikiLeaks?

Are sanctuaries in this country under surveillance as suspected meeting places for anti-American activities? Can anyone remember the last time the Immigration and Naturalization Service burst into an American church looking for illegal immigrants and were met at the door by a congregational mob chanting, "Take them, and you'll have to take us all! There are no strangers here!"

No. American Christians, by and large, have exactly the opposite reputation. Our support for the illegal invasion of Iraq, for example, outpaced support from the general population. The more secular the protestor, the more likely he or she was to be marching in the streets; the more "Christian," the less likely. Pulpits fell silent, and media outlets called dissenters "bad Americans." Outside the walls of organized religion, however, people around the world were organizing and participating in the largest mass demonstrations in the history of humanity. It gives new meaning to the word *sanctuary*.

It was our Christian sisters and brothers who formed the base of support for retributive violence after 9/11, and why should this be a surprise? One's view of God and the mechanics of salvation as requiring the shedding of innocent blood cannot help but justify what Walter Wink called the "myth of redemptive violence."

The judgment of so many Christians against our gay sisters and brothers is more vitriolic and sexually obsessed than among those who do not describe themselves as religious at all. Church meeting spaces are so often, in practice at least, the last bastions of white privilege and theological exclusiveness. Woe to the preacher who resists that empire—the Imperia of Male Caucasian Entitlement. We pray every Sunday, "*Your* kingdom come, *your* will be done," but what we whisper under our breath is, "*My* kingdom stay, *my* will be done." For millions, Jesus is not a change agent at all, but a kind of *neutral energy*, a spiritual additive, like STP—something we pour into our individual tanks so we will get wherever we are going faster and with fewer knocks. But who dares to ask the obvious question: Where are we going?

Were It Not for Artists

Resistance to empire never comes from the established order. It comes from artists. It bubbles up in their poetry; it leaks off their canvas; it slips past the censors who come to close the show and then fell fast asleep in the theater. There are actually people alive today who still think that Ronald Reagan and Margaret Thatcher brought down the iron curtain. Not so. It was the poets in Prague who did it.

It starts with cups of thick coffee and the irrepressible imagination of the young. It grows organically from what is whispered in the heart and then shouted from the rooftops. Indeed, institutions are seldom responsible for change. Individuals seized by a vision are the catalyst. One remembers a local boy from Nazareth whose turn at reading the text changed the world: "Today this scripture has been fulfilled in your hearing" (Lk. 4:21).

Come to think of it, why should the elites today, the rich and powerful, hear the cries of the poor? They never have. As the Psalmist put it, "they have no pain; their bodies are sound and sleek. They are not in trouble as others are; they are not plagued like other people. Therefore pride is their necklace; violence covers them like a garment. Their eyes swell out with fatness; their hearts overflow with follies" (Ps. 73:4–7).

So where does one go looking for truth today, and the courage to "speak truth to power"? Where is the voice of lamentation in our time, Rachel weeping for her children shot to death in their own schools with a grotesque and demonic regularity? Or what about the daily drive-by carnage in our poorest neighborhoods? Where are today's prophets? Are they so eccentric that they look and sound like fools for God? If the church is just another place to worship guns and nurture communities of fear, then we would be better off without it. When did you last hear a good sermon on "what the NRA hath wrought"?

To fall off the horse of empire is to fall a long, long way, but to keep riding it with an assault weapon in one hand and a cross in the other is an absurdity. Who will deliver us from our deadly illusions? For help, we turn one last time to the poetry of Anna Kamieńska. This one is called "The Weariness of the Prophet Elijah."

Lord
You understand such immense weariness
when one only whispers
release your servant now
deliver me from the scraps of hunger and thirst
called life
I don't need more than
the shade of a broom-tree to rest my head
a shawl of darkness for my eyes
Call back the angel
who hastens with bread and a jar of water
Send me a long purifying sleep
childless
Lift my loneliness above its burden
above every bereavement
Lord
You know the weariness of your prophets
You wake them with a jolt of new pain
to place a new desert beneath their feet
to give them a new mouth a new voice
and a new name[10]

I chose this poem because, quite frankly, it fairly drips with weariness. When someone asks me to describe the church in our time, the first word that comes to mind is *weary*. The clergy seem weary. Denominational officials seem weary. Even dedicated volunteers who give so much of their time and talent to their churches seem weary. A kind of spiritual fatigue seems to hover over us as we shrink in size and influence. Maybe the poet is right; maybe we need a new mouth, a new voice, and a new name.

No Politics from the Pulpit, Please

Clergy are being asked to do the impossible, caught between the incendiary gospel they are commissioned to preach, teach, and act upon in the world, and the narrow confines of what the average congregation (or at least the ever-present vocal minority that controls most congregations) considers appropriate speech and acceptable mission. I spoke to the annual meetings of the UCC in Vermont and Massachusetts recently, and a minister came up to me after a sermon on the healing of the paralytic and told me that she was the one who felt paralyzed. Upon being called to her new church, the first thing she was told by the governing board was that she was forbidden to make any reference in any sermon to anything that could be considered "political."

I wondered how she was expected to preach at all, given that the broad definition of politics (Who has the power? How is it exercised? To what effect?) makes almost everything Jesus said and did political. Or, to put it another way, the clergy can be apolitical only when public policy becomes a victimless crime. Preachers can be ordered to stay out of politics only when those in power cease to exercise it in a way that either makes things better or worse for the people for whom Christ died.

Never mind that the Bible is, from start to finish, a story of rebellion—from the divine punishment and promise of Genesis, through the revolutionary message of Jesus against Roman family values and legalistic religion, to Paul and his vision of inclusion, and finally to John and his misunderstood apocalypse. It was all about resisting the status quo. We owe the existence of scripture itself to scribes who resisted the idea that we should ever forget what happened, and so copied it by candlelight. They must also have hidden some gospels considered "heretical," to avoid persecution.

"Do not be conformed to this world, but be transformed
by the renewing of your minds, so that you may discern what
is the will of God—what is good and acceptable and perfect"
(Romans 12:2). This may be the most dangerous verse in the
Bible, because conformity is what comes naturally to us. If such
nonconformity were again to become a non-negotiable spiritual discipline (rather than just a theme for the Beecher Lectures), the Jesus People would constitute an unacceptable threat
to the empire. Resistance would not be a "quarterly emphasis"
or a "mission moment," but a way of life. Instead of a fringe
idea for a few hardcore social gospel types (those renegades that
form the dissident Sunday school class meeting in a room as
far away from the minister's office as possible), nonconformity
would be our faithful response to the coming of the kingdom.
And what sort of company would we be keeping? For starters,
it was for precisely such resistance that Rome crucified
Jesus of Nazareth, executed Paul of Tarsus, and exiled John of
Patmos.

The Trouble with Tranquility

Meanwhile, in the body of Christ today people insist that
clergy not make trouble, that we keep it polite, that visitors see
the interior décor of our churches as "lovely." Our meeting
agendas are often dominated by such urgent business as
whether or not to allow the teenagers to eat pizza in the parlor,
or what shade of white to paint the sanctuary. By all means, says
the "church growth" crowd, do not run off your biggest con-
tributors by telling them what you really learned in seminary.
Instead, adopt the politically correct marketing strategies that
are successful in the empire. The ministerial staff should "sell"
the benefits of church to "customers" who are hard to satisfy

but easy to offend. Membership will then become as easy as our preaching must remain vacuous.

I am not suggesting that we make people take two years of theological training before they are baptized, as did those in the early church. Nor am I suggesting that once we are baptized we should also refuse to wear the uniform of any army. But otherwise, how would anyone know that "Onward Christian Soldiers" is a theological contradiction? Just ponder this: we went from *no* Christians could be soldiers in the second century to *only* Christians could be Roman soldiers in the fourth century.

This is no small change, any more than it is to consider that in the Sermon on the Mount, there is not a single word about what to believe, only words about what to *do* and how to *be* in the world. Yet in just a few hundred years, that radical ethic would be subsumed by the great creeds, in which there is not a single word about what to do, or how to be in the world, but *only* words about what to believe.

Once, when a group of us were studying with the great Presbyterian preacher Ernest Campbell, he summed up this move from Christianity as a way of being in the world to a belief system in a most unforgettable way. He handed out copies of the Apostles' Creed and told us to look carefully at the first few lines, including the punctuation, which we did.

"Where exactly," Campbell asked, "is the life of Jesus in the Apostles' Creed?" We were confused, so he asked again, "Where is the *life* of Jesus—the teaching, the healing, the forgiving, the acts of mercy and compassion? Look closely at the creed," he said, "and tell me where you find it."

After a long, awkward silence, one student finally raised her hand and said, "I guess it's somewhere in the line, 'born of the Virgin Mary, suffered under Pontius Pilate. . .'"

"That's correct," said Campbell. "Jesus is born and then he suffers. All that stands between the two is a comma. Here is the world's most important life reduced to a comma."

At the time I had no way of knowing that years later my own denomination, the United Church of Christ, would launch a marketing campaign that centered on the comma. UCC ministers would even wear tiny red commas on their lapels. The idea came from that unlikely theologian Gracie Allen, who said: "Never place a period where God has placed a comma. God is still speaking."

Lately, we have extended the campaign to include the slogan "Live the comma." We mean, of course, to listen for the still-speaking voice of God, which the comma encourages but a period closes. But in Campbell's example, the meaning is deeper and more disturbing than we realized. In an age when Christianity is still largely defined by creeds, the comma is all that is left of Jesus!

Preaching as an Act of Resistance

Again, how do we know that discipleship is grounded in resistance and not beliefs? For one thing, the Lord never says, "Go and *believe* likewise." We can argue over the extent to which specific events in the New Testament are historical, quasi-historical, or outright fictions created to fulfill Old Testament prophesies or ratify archetypal Jewish themes. But what we overlook in this search for the "truth" (defined as post-Enlightenment veracity) is how consistently the whole story constitutes a meta-narrative of rebellion.

Take the first sermon preached by Jesus in his home synagogue at Nazareth. It begins well enough—a local boy takes his turn as worship leader. He follows the custom of standing to read Torah and sitting to interpret it. But he chooses Isaiah, and the prophet's announcement of the reign of God: good news for the poor, release to the captives, and recovery of sight to the blind. He must have been a good public speaker, since the response was (I'm paraphrasing now): *Nice job. Well spoken. Mary, you must be proud.*

What follows, however, is pure resistance. Past and future tense become present tense. The time is *now*; the scripture is fulfilled in your hearing. The psychological subtext: *Sure, I look ordinary, but that's because no prophet is accepted in the prophet's hometown.* Or to put it in current vernacular, "You all say, 'Amen, good sermon, Reverend,' and then try to beat the Baptists to brunch, believing that you are sanctified."

What about the time of Elijah when there was a famine, and you did nothing? Only a widow at Zarephath in Sidon received mercy. Or the time of Elisha, when so many needed healing but only one was cleansed, Naaman the Syrian? Needless to say, the rhetorical love fest was over, because as Peter Gomes put it, "[Jesus] unacceptably collapsed piety and policy into a single obligation."[11]

This is exactly what the church must do now—*collapse piety and policy into a single obligation.* Why? Because the primary illusion of our time is that faith can be personally redemptive without being socially responsible. Nobody knows this better than Pope Francis. He followed a keeper of dogma in a time of scandal with the fresh wind of the spirit of compassion personified. Resisting pomp and grandeur in the spirit of a servant, he restored the spirit of the resister from Nazareth.

You see, prophets always do the same thing regardless of their religious tradition. They lift up the text that presumes to define us and say: *This is what we say we are.* Then they lay it alongside a portrait of reality: *This is what we really are.* Then

they ask: *So what's wrong with this picture?* This is exactly what
Dr. King did on the steps of the Lincoln Memorial in 1963. Here
is what our Constitution says we are: "created equal" (our national text). Here is the reality of segregation (what we really
are). So what's wrong with this picture?

To their credit, African American churches have always
understood the gospel as resistance, especially to slavery, and
then later against a continuing second-class status after
emancipation. Indeed, the white church has much to learn from
how clear and resounding is the tradition of prophetic black
Christianity.[12]

Jesus Was Anti-Temple

The ministry of Jesus was anti-Temple from day one. He
preaches only one indoor sermon, and it doesn't end well. His
only recorded return to the center of religious life in Jerusalem
was to attack it as a den of robbers and thieves, an offense worthy of crucifixion all by itself. The empire was using the Temple-
state as an instrument of imperial control. It allowed Rome to
seem benevolent in providing for the worship of Israel's God
while providing economic support for a priestly aristocracy
that both controlled the area and rendered tribute to the empire.

Herod had vastly expanded the Temple complex in a bid
to make it one of the seven wonders of the Roman imperial
world. But to finance such an enormous undertaking, he had
to collect more in taxes, which added more debt to an already
impoverished agrarian class. "It should not be surprising
that the Gospels and other sources represent Jesus and other
prophets as addressing conditions of hunger and debt."[13]

Hunger and debt? Does this sound familiar? They are the
twin demons of poverty. Yet the illusion continues, says Richard

Horsley, that the subject matter of the Bible is religion, not politics and economics. "In addition, modern Western individualism led to the idea that Jesus and the Pauline letters were addressing individual faith and morality, and not communities, peoples, and institutional structures."[14]

Walter Brueggemann put it another way, speaking about the eternal battle between those who run the pyramid schemes of wealth and power and those who care about the neighborhood. That's why the Sabbath is not about being "religious" but about "work stoppage" that withdraws us from the anxiety system of Pharaoh. When we are taught to be compassionate as a religious obligation, this is not something we practice in isolation from systems that harm. It is instead a "radical form of criticism, for it announces that the hurt is to be taken seriously, that the hurt is not to be accepted as normal and natural but is an abnormal and unacceptable condition for humanness."[15]

The Jewish prophets warned Israel to resist such illusions. Hosea said that God had a "lawsuit against Israel," and "therefore the land mourns, and all who live in it languish; together with the wild animals and the birds of the air, even the fish of the sea are perishing" (Hosea 4:3).

Where is such brave poetry today? Where is this spirit of resistance in the age of global climate change? Early American voices for wilderness conservation like John Muir and Aldo Leopold gave way to the more urgent voices of Rachel Carson's *Silent Spring*. Now, with the exception of Wendell Berry, Bill McKibben, and a handful of others, the pulpit is largely silent on the destruction of the environment. Christian evangelicals, on the other hand, have cornered the market on those who deny the reality of global climate change altogether.

Yet the land does indeed mourn; the birds of the air and the fish are indeed perishing. Yet we drill deeper (and now horizontally) to satisfy our addiction to fossil fuel without a clue as to what the long-term consequences will be. We violate the neighborhood by turning it into a truck stop. The voice of the prophets is the voice of resistance, reminding us that not to act is to act. The ways of life and death have been put before us, so choose life. Our present illusion, however—still riding the horse of empire—is that life can be both a game of *Monopoly* and a neighborhood of human communion and covenant relationships.

Nibbling at Scripture Is Not Enough

Thanks to the work of postcolonial scholars, we can now see resistance to empire in many of the texts that we had previously sentimentalized into irrelevance. Part of our problem, of course, is that on any given Sunday morning we read only tiny slices of scripture in worship, usually from the lectionary. "Pericopes," we call them, and they hardly give us the sweep and scope of resistance to empire that is so powerfully represented in the gospel of Mark, for example—especially when we hear it from start to finish—when someone "performs" Mark on stage to sold-out audiences.

As a result of our post-Enlightenment understanding of truth, scholars isolate individual sayings of Jesus as if the "historical Jesus" can be most fully glimpsed this way. Alas, what is lost is the context that ultimately gives all those individual sayings their meaning. One scholar gives a helpful example of why we could not be expected to understand the "historical" Martin Luther King, Jr., by focusing mainly on his speeches:

> We would have only a very limited sense of King
> if we focused only on his speeches. To adequately

understand the historical figure of King we cannot separate him from the civil rights movement of which he was a principal leader. And we cannot understand King and the civil rights movement unless we know American history, particularly the history of slavery, emancipation of slaves, and reconstruction and segregation in the South; unless we understand the sharp cultural conflict between American and Christian ideals and the harsh realities of slavery and segregation. And we cannot understand how King and the civil rights movement formed and operated unless we know about African American churches as the principal political as well as religious base of African American communities, in which people began to get organized and in which the role of the preacher provided the model that was adapted by King and his followers as the civil rights movements developed.[16]

The gospel of Mark has been called a passion narrative with a long introduction. It is also from start to finish a vortex of resistance. After announcing the arrival of the kingdom, Jesus begins to heal everyone in sight, but with hidden messages as well. After exorcising a whole "legion" of demons from the Gerasene demoniac, the demons must be "parked" somewhere lest they find others to possess. What better place to put homeless demons than in a herd of swine? Then the pigs proceed to self-destruct.

I thought for years that this was just a rather bizarre tale of possessed porkers, or "deviled ham." In fact, the clue lies in the word "legion," the name for a Roman army unit. Not only does foreign occupation and oppression drive people crazy (and create more terrorists than it kills, to use a modern analogy), but for all those who live under occupation, the dream is that one day the occupying legions will self-destruct, as do all empires.

In the story of two women healed, the daughter of Jairus, near to death, and the woman who had been hemorrhaging for twelve years but manages to touch the hem of Jesus's cloak, there is a metaphor for occupied Israel—being bled dry and almost dead, but still seeking deliverance.

A wealthy man is deluded into thinking that he has kept the Mosaic Law but is so in love with his wealth that Jesus declares it nearly impossible for a rich man to enter the kingdom. In a refrain of the prophetic tradition, the warning is as clear as it is so often ignored: *if wealth is life's only object, then death will follow.*

A widow offers her mite to enter the Temple, but instead of a tale of indignation about charging the poor a kind of "toll" to enter the Temple (a tribute for Yahweh?), modern pulpits have softened it into a lesson about generosity, usually to encourage stewardship during the annual pledge drive. Meanwhile, Jesus the spiritual insurgent disappears, frozen in stained glass.

Death, Taxes, and Lampooning the Empire

Perhaps the most dramatic story of resistance to empire in the New Testament comes when Jesus is asked about the payment of taxes (or the tribute) to Caesar. The Pharisees ask Jesus a straightforward question: Is it lawful to pay taxes to the emperor or not? They know very well that according to the covenantal commandments it is not, but as client rulers they are also the ones responsible to collect it. It is a trap. If Jesus says yes, it is lawful to pay the tribute, he would lose credibility as a prophet of the people; if he says no, Rome would consider this tantamount to rebellion and send in the troops.

His response is to ask for a coin and then to ask the famous (or infamous) question, "Whose head is this, and whose title?" When the obvious answer is given, he says something that everyone present would have understood: "Give therefore to the emperor the things that are the emperor's, and to God the things that are God's" (Matt. 22:21). Without being trapped, he nevertheless got the message across. Why? Because what really belongs to Rome? The answer: nothing. What really belongs to God? The answer: everything.

When seen through Western eyes, however, such stories are heard as the defense of the separation of church and state, or as a "gotcha moment" in the battle between Jesus and the Pharisees. Lost is the deeper truth: this is a direct challenge to imperial power. What's more, the power to tax is perhaps the empire's greatest and most resented power. In recent American history, tax cuts have favored the rich at the expense of the poor. As the gap between rich and poor widens to levels never seen before, preachers can resist by talking about economic democracy again, and a new economy based on jubilee justice.[17]

What we cannot afford to do, however, is keep retelling Bible stories as if they were harmless, apolitical episodes. For example, when the Lord enters Jerusalem for the last time, he stages perhaps the most transparent lampoon of the imperial power in the gospel. He enters on a donkey, fulfilling the vision of Zechariah, but the scene is no "triumphal entry," as I was taught in Sunday school—a messianic coronation with a handsome, smiling Jesus adorning the cover of the Palm Sunday bulletin.

Little did I know (because preachers never told me) that no respectable conqueror enters the city except through opened gates, or at worst through shattered walls, but either way riding on a battle chariot or on a war horse, not on a donkey. In my mind, I see his chalky legs dangling down to scrape the ground while all the unwashed "you peoples" of the world scream their heads off.

Scholars also believe that this was not the only parade to enter the city that day. From the west, a "troop surge" of Roman soldiers was making its prescribed visit to the city led by Pilate to remind the people what a real military parade looks like: row upon row of Roman cavalry, with helmets, weapons, and golden eagles on poles glinting in the sunlight.

Meanwhile, from the east side comes the resister of empire staging the "un-parade," the anti-triumphal entry, the anti-imperial spectacle to dramatize the alternative to retributive violence and peace through victory. Needless to say, Rome was not amused, any more than we are amused today by the likes of Army private Bradley Manning of Crescent, Oklahoma. He defected from the empire by leaking the secrets of empire, including the infamous "murder video" that showed the world with what indiscriminant machismo the "good guys" can also murder and make jokes about it as if playing a video game.

Or consider Edward Snowden, the former intelligence analyst for the empire who leaked massive amounts of data to prove that all of us were being (are being) spied on. Whether you call these men whistleblowers or traitors depends a lot on how much you trust the empire to protect you and to police itself. If you are not much worried, then I fear you are not much a student of history.

So let me say it this way: If the Body of Christ has become just one more peculiar gathering of the loyal subjects of empire, singing and praying for the success of the empire, then we have no Good News to offer, just religious propaganda. If we allow ourselves to be intimidated in our search for truth by the gate-keepers of empire—the billionaires who are now buying up all our newspapers and television stations in order to report from the corporate mountaintop news that is so fake that a whole generation now gets its real news from fake news programs, then we are all wandering in the wilderness. By the way, would that more preachers of the gospel had the fearlessness of Jon Stewart.

So Let's Get Started

Enough talk of rebellion. Where does the rebellion itself begin? Here are four steps for clergy to begin a kind of spiritual mutiny, to return The Way to the ways of defiance. First, *we take all of the American flags out of our sanctuaries*, where they most certainly do not belong. Put them in the fellowship hall to represent our proud tradition of democracy, but don't display them in that sacred space set aside to be "a house of prayer for all people."

Second, *let's admit to loving, but being captured by, our tax-exempt status*. We cannot take government subsidies and then presume to be independent contractors for the gospel. So-called faith-based initiatives are a bad idea. Churches should not be tax exempt, and preachers should not get special tax breaks. This will be opposed by every American denomination in the country on behalf of starving clergy. But deep down, we know that we are selling our souls. Besides, let's be honest and admit that *most of our churches are empty all week*, which begs the question: What are we returning in service to our communities on behalf of the common good that *justifies* our tax exemption in the first place?

Third, *we could keep the Sabbath again*. Not out of some puritanical misconception about so-called blue laws, but so that we might protest with our rest the idea that "no rest but death" is how the empire defines working hard enough. We can't even stay home for an entire day on Thanksgiving now, but must return to the stores at sundown for Black Friday Eve. It was Brueggemann who said, "Sabbath, in the first instance, is not about worship. It is about work stoppage. It is about withdrawal from the anxiety system of Pharaoh, the refusal to let one's life be defined by production and consumption and the endless pursuit of private well-being."[18] Just imagine the power of millions of Christians who refuse to shop when we are supposed to be resting and grateful.

Fourth, *we should cherish and strictly observe the separation of church and state.* It was the measured genius of our founding fathers to give us both freedom *of* religion and freedom *from* religion. We often take it for granted when it is useful to us, and ignore it with impunity when it isn't. Whenever possible, individual religious choices and expressions should be honored, even celebrated. But not at the expense of the common good or the religious freedom of those who work for corporations. The religious beliefs of the owners of for-profit enterprises do not trump the religious beliefs of their workers, despite recent Supreme Court rulings. The clergy should resist being "used" by local and state governments who ask for prayers to open meetings, and preachers should never endorse candidates from the pulpit or distribute campaign literature or "voter guides."

There are more steps to consider, of course, like lending money to members of the Beloved Community at no interest, making the church a safe place for conscientious objectors as well as soldiers, and being a sanctuary of last resort for migrant workers (illegal or otherwise). The rich and powerful dominate the decision-making process (locally and nationally) unless advocates for the poor and marginalized show up at city council meetings en masse. The people of The Way need to get involved in *community organizing*, setting aside the most intractable issues like abortion and gay marriage to focus on hunger, education, public transportation, criminal justice, and health care. Most of the ground is common ground.

People are not fleeing churches today because they have lost their deep hunger for a spiritual connection and participation in authentic spiritual communities. Rather, they are fleeing because so many churches now seem bereft of the very spirit that birthed them in the first place. If clergy want to find their people, they might try looking in coffee shops, in homeless shelters, among the young who have pitched their tents in parks to dramatize economic injustice. While we shop, salute, and worship celebrities and athletes, the world is falling apart. What we need today is a move to *Occupy Religion*.[19]

The spirit will move with or without us. Somewhere at this very moment the church is being reborn by a movement of that spirit that blows where it will, and not by a denominational initiative or a new church marketing strategy. It happens when followers "go and do likewise." A disciple knows joy and experiences clarity only by *doing* the gospel, not as the by-product of a slick campaign to get the gospel done. It is true what they say: fewer and fewer people care much about denominations or ecclesiology these days. They do, however, want to feel the hair stand up on the back of their necks.

Needless to say, a church open to the movement of the spirit is as unpredictable as it is irresistible. But this is not how bishops and church growth planners understand the religious impulse. They seek order while the spirit seeks creative disorder. In Greek mythology, the spirit is like Dionysus, but the church is like Apollo. The former creates chaos and disorder, while the latter seeks order, calm, clarity, and beauty. Institutions by nature try to manage Dionysian truth by making it fit into a controlled Apollonian order. It must be this way, but it also can spell death for those churches that forget that the insurgent spirit must always trump institutional order.

As America "browns," Western churches are for many a white refuge, where a white Jesus hovers over a white, well-dressed crowd. There are not many day laborers in mainline churches, but lots of overmedicated suburbanites. They sit in the antiseptic splendor of rooms built for comfort, while hovering above them are equally antiseptic statues of a hairless and radiant Jesus—floating weightless above the real world like the blue man in the Chagall.

This is the Jesus of guilt and predatory capitalism, a.k.a. the patron saint of wealthy white men (arguably the most dangerous single class of humans on the planet). This is the Chamber of Commerce Jesus who winks at whatever the market will bear instead of telling us that whatever the market will bear has become unbearable. So *for the love of God, resist!*

Come to think of it, I like the sound of that. So much so that I asked those who first heard this lecture at Yale to join me in a call and response, and they did so with gusto. Readers can join in as well. It's simple. When I say, "For the love of God" you say out loud to yourself, "RESIST!" You can even try reading it in a group, and ask listeners to stomp their feet for added emphasis.

For the Love of God, RESIST!

- There will be no renewal of the church until we risk being subversive again for the cause of love. In a time when everything is for sale, when the common good seems like a quaint idea instead of a moral imperative, and when yet another white man can shoot dead another unarmed black teenager and get away with murder, I say, *for the love of God* . . . RESIST!

- In a land where many of us condemn one president for acting like a cowboy but look the other way when the current occupant of the White House orders more drone strikes than any president in history, mocking our Constitution and killing the innocent—I say, *for the love of God* . . . RESIST!

- When on the Fourth of July, in addition to our standard military parades, churches might want to consider having the youth group make "un-floats" for the "un-parade." Something powered by a donkey perhaps, entered under the previously unknown category of nonviolent restorative justice. The press would love it. Even that cable news network named after Herod the Fox would have a field day. Imagine the commentary of the talking heads: "The Christians staged their own parade for peace today. Here they are wearing garlands, releasing white doves, and carrying some unidentified object, not sure what that it is." The reporter responds, "That's a pruning hook"; the anchor responds, "Whatever." So what if we gave a war and nobody came? I say, *for the love of God* . . . RESIST!

- Not long ago, the most important and frightening story ever to run in the *New York Times* appeared. It was a report on the unanimous verdict of climate scientists using special atmospheric measuring equipment in Hawaii to conclude, without a doubt, that the level of carbon dioxide trapped in that life-giving sliver of air above us now exceeds the dreaded four hundred parts per million. The train has left the station, and all we can do now is try to slow it down, and prepare ourselves for the consequences. But one thing we will not do is "shoot the messenger" or pretend that God can't communicate with us through science, but only through anti-intellectual piety. I come from a part of the world in which too many people still think that there is something endearing about ignorance. Many such souls have found safe haven in the church (and in Washington). But there is nothing—absolutely nothing—"endearing" about ignorance. Ignorance is dangerous. So, can the church please clear its throat and join me in saying, *for the love of God* . . . RESIST!

- Years ago, William Sloane Coffin, Jr., came to visit Phillips Theological Seminary in Oklahoma, where I was a student and about to be ordained. He shocked and angered us all when he said that he believed that in the next thirty years (and that was thirty years ago) America might very well become *fascist*. We were in the chapel, for heaven's sake, and a few students crossed their arms over their chests in discomfort, while at least one trustee walked out. That's an ugly word, evoking the horrors of the Third Reich and the Holocaust and jack-booted thugs—except that Coffin went on to explain that this was not what he was talking about. Rather, he said, "I mean to apply the broad, classical definition of fascism in Western culture." A student raised his hand to ask, "So what is the definition?" And Bill said, "Control of the government by special inter-ests with the blessing of the church." If that sounds like a prediction that came true, then I say, *for the love of God* . . . RESIST!

- That was 1979, during the Iranian hostage crisis, and not a single one of us could have dreamed that some day the

Supreme Court would rule that corporations are people. In what may be the worst ruling since Dred Scott, *Citizens United* merely capped a trend in which an increasingly unregulated financial sector is becoming, and now is, more powerful than government. So I have come among you to ask a serious question. Who will tell us the truth if our preachers are muzzled? It is a victory for the empire, but not for the kingdom of God, that if you are "too big to fail" it means that your rewards are privatized but your risks are socialized. You can gamble with other people's money, and if you win, you win. But if you lose, *we* lose. I don't know what economic model that is, but it's not God's economy, so I say, *for the love of God* . . . RESIST!

- Don't just march and chant and then go home. The empire loves it when we blow off steam. It proves we "live in a democracy" and "people have the right to express themselves" (at least in "free speech zones" a thousand feet away from anyone in power). But when someone says "boycott" or cuts up their credit card and refuses to do business with banks that are a criminal enterprise, corporations get as nervous as long-tailed cats in a room full of rocking chairs. So I say, consume with your conscience, and *for the love of God* . . . RESIST!

- Now that fifty years have passed since the March on Washington, I invite you to look once more at those grainy black-and-white films of that amazing nonviolent gathering on the National Mall. What you will notice, as all those people come streaming off the buses they have ridden for hours, is *what they are wearing.* They are all dressed for church. Why? Because they saw what they were doing as going to church. So I say to all you well-dressed people, *for the love of God* . . . RESIST!

- Have we forgotten how much of the Hebrew scripture
  sought to build a wall between greed and the people
  who are trampled by it? Again and again, the Bible tells
  us that "God is a God of 'justice and righteousness,' and
  that redundant expression names God as a God of
  distributive justice who does what is right by doing what
  is just, and does what is just by doing what is right."[20]
  And how exactly is this accomplished? By *regulations*
  that are intended to be instruments of divine justice.
  God degrees that "the land shall not be sold in perpetu-
  ity, for the land is mine; with me you are but aliens and
  tenants" (Lev. 25:23). Since land is life, it should not fall
  into the hands of the few, the 1 percent, because land is
  no ordinary economic commodity. Instead of buying
  up more as if "enough is never enough," the writer of
  Deuteronomy warns, "You must not move your neighbor's boundary marker, set up by former generations,
  on the property that will be allotted to you in the land
  that the Lord your God is giving you to possess" (Deut.
  19:14). Now that so few own so much and so many have
  so little, I say, *for the love of God . . .* RESIST!
- Charging interest is forbidden among those who lend
  under the Torah, so what would happen, I wonder, if
  the church were to return to this ancient practice, and
  begin to lend money again to its members at no interest? It might be the greatest incentive to church membership since Paul told Gentile men they could convert
  without having to cut off the end of their penis! It is
  our *biblical heritage* to control collateral, cancel debts,
  reverse dispossession, free the slaves of debt, and in the
  crowning act of God's economy, observe a Jubilee every
  fifty years, where all land and property shall be returned

to its original owners. Can you imagine anything more un-American than the cancellation of debt? Yet debt can be a form of indentured servitude, a form of slavery—so I say, *for the love of God . . .* RESIST!

- If there are rules against taking advantage of resident aliens, then why are so many Christians the first to call for deportation of migrants? It's as if we expect these strangers to provide us with cheap manual labor, roofing our houses, landscaping our yards, pouring concrete, and caring for our children, but then we want them to disappear after sundown. And since it is forbidden in scripture to "take a widow's garment in pledge," why on earth do we allow the pawnshop and payday loan industries to operate among us with impunity? These people are vultures circling over the roadkill of poverty. We are supposed to have a "preferential option for the poor," but they certainly don't get preferential rates! So I say, *for the love of God . . .* RESIST!

- How is it that we can remain silent when our society claims to love children (they are the future, you know), when obviously we love them only in theory? How do we know this? Just look around. We have the finest sport complexes and the worst public schools in the developed world. So I say, *for the love of God . . .* RESIST!

- On behalf of women, without whom no church that I know of could possibly exist—those who were last at the cross and first at the tomb, but who are still not equal citizens in the kingdom—I say, *for the love of God . . .* RESIST!

- On behalf of our gay/lesbian/bisexual/transgendered sisters and brothers, can we not find room at the Lord's Table by remembering that it is not our table to begin with? I say, with Pope Francis, that we call a truce on arguments over abortion and gay marriage long enough to remember that the gospel is about being loving, not about being right. So if you believe that no one should ever have an abortion under any circumstances, then under no circumstances should you ever have an abortion. But let's not make that decision for every other woman in every circumstance in which she may find herself pregnant. If you do not believe in gay marriage, then just refrain from marrying a gay person (just say no). But by all means, let us not allow the government to tell adults whom they can love or how they can love. So I say, *for the love of God* . . . RESIST!

- To the best-selling atheists of our time, who have lumped us all together into one ridiculous religious cartoon and then proudly announce that they don't believe in the God that most of us don't believe in either, I say, *for the love of God* . . . RESIST!

- When someone on the street asks you a simple question, like "What is the first step to becoming a Christian?" you could be ready with a simple assignment rather than a list of doctrines. You could say, "When you are standing in line in the grocery store and you see a young black man who is sacking your groceries and avoiding your gaze, then wait until he meets it and say, 'Thank you, *sir*.'" You could put in a garden so you won't forget where food really comes from. Raise nonviolent children, and remember the gospel truth: not a single one of us gets out of this life alive, all families are dysfunctional, and either all of us matter or none of us do. So to all those who say that only *some* of us do, I say, *for the love of God* . . . RESIST!

- Mute the soundtrack of the empire and its incessant babble and talk a walk. Read more poetry. Figure out how to be alone with yourself and not go to the bar looking for a hookup. We really are what we do when no one is looking. And please help us to recover the sacred vocabulary of our faith, because some of our most important words have been stolen—words like "crisis." The empire wants you to believe that a quarterback with a sore arm is a "crisis" because he may not be able to start in the big game. Can the church of Jesus Christ be the first to say it, please? A quarterback with a sore arm is *not* a crisis. It is a quarterback with a sore arm. We know what a real crisis is. A crisis is a father with four kids and no job. It's a mother whose husband beats her and then abandons her, and now she shoots up in front of her kids to make it through the day. Because we do know what a real crisis is, I say, *for the love of God . . .* RESIST!

- Finally, we have our own crisis in the church to worry about. It is Holy Scripture written by the calloused hands of the oppressed now stroked in worship by the manicured hands of the Oppressor. It is disciples of The Way trying so hard to fit in with popular culture that we have lost the capacity to critique that culture. A crisis is the loss of the sacred feminine, the forgotten value of art, and juvenile definitions of manhood in a culture without enough grown-up fathers. A crisis is a congregation that goes to church to be entertained, but so infrequently hears the radical gospel of Jesus Christ that in a moment of painful clarity, instead of applauding, each might turn to the other and say: *We are undone!* A real crisis is a terrible thing to waste, so I say, *for the love of God . . .* RESIST!

To close, let it be said that we have spoken of important things and did not blink. But let it also be said that talking about it guarantees nothing. To get it done, we must first be "undone." To resist ego, orthodoxy, and empire can be accomplished only by the gift of a fearless faith, one that shatters all our illusions, one that knocks us off our horse, one that allows us to be led, like blind Saul to Damascus.

The poet knows what we need:

Lord
You know the weariness of your prophets
You wake them with a jolt of new pain
to place a new desert beneath their feet
to give them a new mouth a new voice
and a new name

May it be so, and may it begin with you and with me.
For if not *us*, then who?
If not *here*, then where?
If not *now*, then when?
We are the leaven that God would hide in the imperial loaf. We are salt and light and seed, and all we have to do is walk straight into that light—the same light that is breaking through these very windows at this very moment. See how it falls on our faces?

Do not turn away. But for the love of God, resist.

Epilogue
Resisting the Reign of the Christian Status Quo

When Martin Luther King, Jr., scribbled his eloquent *Letter from Birmingham Jail* on the margins of a newspaper, he saved his most scathing criticism for "go slow" white clergy and status quo Christians. They "have remained silent behind the anesthetizing security of stained-glass windows," mouthing "pious irrelevancies and sanctimonious trivialities."

Best known as a forceful and deeply biblical defense of nonviolent direct action, King's letter was also driven by a deep personal frustration. When one's colleagues in ministry fail to step up and recognize the "urgency of the moment," it is more painful than outright resistance from one's enemies. We face a similar moment in the church today that encompasses far more than race, which still bedevils us. With few exceptions, the clergy are among the most timid and cloistered of voices in a time of convulsive change.

We need to remember important lessons from the civil rights movement. In the midst of a campaign to desegregate public accommodations in Birmingham, Alabama, King had

decided to be arrested himself when the movement flagged and
stalling tactics were proving effective. On Good Friday, 1963, he
and Ralph Abernathy led a march in violation of a city injunc-
tion against such protests, and both men were tossed into a
police van and sent to solitary confinement.

While there, his mind sharpened by the solitude of a "narrow jail cell," King was handed a copy of a newspaper in which
eight of Alabama's prominent religious leaders had issued a
statement, a "Call for Unity," that attacked the campaign as
"unwise and untimely." Writing in what one scholar called a
"controlled fury," King laid out not only a defense of moral
resistance to immoral laws, but also a sermon on "the shortcomings of timid moderation in the face of injustice, a sermon of
chastisement—a shrewd, tough-minded, even militant political
document."[1]

Fifty years later, King's letter so aptly describes the malaise
of the church in our time that many have been tempted (myself
included) to petition to have it included as the last book of the
Bible in place of Revelation. What clergyperson cannot relate
to King's deep disappointment in what he called the "white
moderate"? Many lines from this manifesto have been quoted,
but too seldom do we hear these:

> I have traveled the length and breadth of Alabama,
> Mississippi and all the other southern states. On
> sweltering summer days and crisp autumn morn-
> ings I have looked at the South's beautiful churches
> with their lofty spires pointing heavenward. I have
> beheld the impressive outlines of her massive reli-
> gious education buildings. Over and over I have
> found myself asking: "What kind of people wor-
> ship here? Who is their God?"[2]

Who is their God indeed? And why do we still confuse comfort and convenience with piety and patriotism? Those who recline on the hearth of privilege have always been "confused" about the various "untimely" insurgencies that rise in opposition to injustice. They seem to come from nowhere. The Occupy movement that recently sprang up in this country in response to economic injustice seemed to baffle even those sitting in the pews. Ironically, some of them had once opposed the war in Vietnam, but they regarded the issues of this generation as less urgent, or their tactics more juvenile. It is deeply in the nature of human beings to be caught unaware by the movement of the spirit, and to counsel caution and moderation in all things. It was not overt resistance by the principalities and the powers that infuriated King, however, but the moral mediocrity of status quo clergy.

The same group of Alabama clergy that published the letter had also published a previous criticism of Governor George Wallace for threatening to refuse to abide by court-ordered desegregation of schools—a move that earned them the scorn of (and even death threats from) militant segregationists. This way they could appear to be on the side of following the law, at least until it could be appealed.

White moderates wanted to have it both ways, appearing to be concerned about law and order, while also protecting their restless and conflicted congregations. By displaying a moral timidity that misrepresents discipleship as a kind of expedient pragmatism, they played on fears of the "outside agitator" and "extremists," tapping into deep-seated fears and stereotypes. King countered that the polemic of "insider" and "outsider" did not apply to the Southern Christian Leadership Conference, and that to be called an extremist is ironic, given that Jesus was an "extremist for love."

What drove King to eloquent sarcasm, however, was the perennial blindness of the religious status quo when it comes to what he called the "myth of time." Time is morally neutral, he wrote, and is often used by people of ill will to stall moments of activism until the "troublemaker" grows weary and gives up. Often the laws that were passed to mollify the protestors in the short run were cosmetic, or not enforced. "Freedom is never voluntarily given by the oppressor; it must be demanded by the oppressed."

Today's mainline church is still run by white moderates, and in some cases among minority churches, by minority moderates. Some subjects are simply taboo today—like criticism of Israel, lest we appear anti-Semitic, or calling for an end to our deadly infatuation with guns. Even the Pope cannot say that the world is terminally afflicted with greed, which it is, without being called a socialist.

Those who defend the status quo because they benefit from it have a power that is notoriously underestimated by those who attempt to change it. Ask young Arabs who dreamed of a democratic spring, only to see it swept into the deepening vortex of the long winter that is Western imperialism versus radical Islam. Ask women around the world who want something as simple as to make their own decisions and provide an education for their daughters, only to see them kidnapped and their schools burned. Ask migrants who do the most backbreaking labor among us, but whose status is kept purposefully in limbo for political gain.

Ask millions of faithful Catholics whether they believe that institutional preservation trumps righteous resistance, even in the face of crimes against children. Whether it is resistance to ego, orthodoxy, or empire, the stumbling block is still our failure to be more devoted to order than to justice, as King put it. We do indeed still prefer a "negative peace which is the absence of tension" to the positive peace that results from the direct action of the Beloved Community.

Is it not still the white moderate, or in African American churches the black moderate, that counsels caution when the LGBT community comes asking to be included in the full sacramental hospitality of the church? Is it not still the white moderate Sunday school teacher who refuses to preach on economic justice because he believes that all talk of money in church is taboo, even as the gap between rich and poor explodes? Is it not still the white moderate "everyman" who participates in the worship of the warrior in a militarized society, blessing the high-tech murder of the "brown ones" in the name of God? Is it not still the white moderate at prayer whose petitions wink at the divine while caressing the status quo? Is it not still the white moderate pastor who hires an ordained woman but seldom lets her preach, damning her with faint praise for her "beautiful work with our children"?

King never speaks of abandoning the church—indeed he speaks of being "nurtured in its bosom." He is troubled most, however, by those who profess the kingdom of God while maintaining the kingdom of privilege. He expected that the white church would see the "justice of our cause and, with deep concern, would serve as the channel through which our just grievances could reach the power structure." That is, King *expected* the church to be a channel of resistance to what was structurally evil about the empire. Instead she also stalled, having borrowed the tactics of empire and now acting like an empire of its own. Listen to the pathos of these lines:

> I have heard numerous southern religious leaders
> admonish their worshipers to comply with a deseg-
> regation decision because it is the law, but I have

longed to hear white ministers declare: "Follow this decree because integration is morally right and because the Negro is your brother." In the midst of blatant injustices inflicted upon the Negro, I have watched white churchmen stand on the sideline and mouth pious irrelevances and sanctimonious trivialities. In the midst of a mighty struggle to rid our nation of racial and economic injustice, I have heard many ministers say: "Those are social issues, with which the gospel has no real concern." And I have watched many churches commit themselves to a completely other worldly religion which makes a strange, un-Biblical distinction between body and soul, between the sacred and the secular.[3]

It is hard to imagine a more relevant refrain. In my thirty-five years of parish ministry I have found the majority of my clergy colleagues to be decent, conscientious, thoughtful, and sincere. But there is scarcely a prophetic bone left in the body of Christ. When I find it, however, it moves me to tears. On a recent visit to the U.S. border with Mexico, I met a committed group of resisters who belong to Good Shepherd UCC in Sahuarita, Arizona. While other churches in the area are preoccupied with the politics of the immigration debate, the people at Good Shepherd find the spots where migrants die in the desert without water. There they build, install, and maintain water stations in response to the biblical mandate that to give a cup of cold water to a thirsty child is its own reward.

There are other stories of courageous congregations, of course—from churches like Riverside and Judson Memorial in New York City; Fountain Street, Grand Rapids, and Plymouth

Congregational UCC in Washington, D.C.; and University Congregational UCC in Seattle. There are churches in the so-called Emergent movement whose theology is evangelical but who create and sustain strong social gospel ministries. And there are African American churches that continue the work of Dr. King by recognizing its contemporary manifestations—especially with regard to debt, the tragedy of absent fathers, and the need to join with others who struggle to achieve a "post-soul" politics.[4]

The underground churches of the future will be post-denominational BELOVED COMMUNITIES that return to their pacifist roots, create alternative economic models, are active in community organizing, adopt and assist local public schools, and practice "guerrilla gardening" to bring fresh, healthy food back to places where fast food is killing a whole generation of children. If they could combine their financial resources to create a kind of church bank, sharing manna instead of breeding it, think what a shudder it would send through Wall Street.

There are Roman Catholic churches that provide vital, compassionate services to illegal immigrants, and interfaith movements beyond the walls of the church that regard state budgets as a theological document—like the Moral March Movement in North Carolina. A campaign on Facebook is not enough. Social change requires that we put our bodies on the line. Mission work in the third world should not be a cover for evangelism and conversion. It should be for the love of God with no strings attached. When we feed, heal, and house the last and the least, all that is "left behind" is amazing grace.

These communities are inspiriting, but they are, sadly, the exception to the rule. Orthodoxy still commands far more time and energy than does orthopraxy, reversing the emphasis of the early church. Modern purity systems built around race, sexuality, and class remain, as does the cult of "traditional family values." Yet when churches succeed today, above all other attributes they practice an "extravagant welcome." It sounds good in theory, but is also guaranteed to increase the discomfort of those who would prefer to sit in church with people who look like they do.

Three qualities have been identified as central to churches that are thriving: hospitality, diversity, and reflection.[5] These qualities were found recently in only 5 to 6 percent of mainline churches, which means that the opposite qualities are the norm in over 90 percent of our churches: inhospitality, homogeneity, and dogmatism. What's more, we don't need a survey to observe that after a divorce, neither partner usually returns to the church they once belonged to as a couple.

In a denial of the biblical message, some mega-churches preach that wholeness, health, and wealth are a sign of God's favor. Hence, when we are broken, sick, and poor, we must be an unworthy candidate for the community first populated by the broken, the sick, and the poor.

We live in a time of empire-sponsored deception on a scale never seen before. Knowing that great wealth for the minority depends upon maintaining the ignorance and powerlessness of the majority, corporations have become our electronic parents, our providers, and the storytellers of the age. First they are ravenous, and second they are masters of propaganda, making sublimely beautiful commercials to persuade us that they are not really in business to make and sell things—but rather to love the earth, its people, and the justice that only the marketplace can bring us.

To save the church we must become radical truth-tellers again: the truth about our addictions, our illusions, and our dysfunctional families. Making disciples is the first order of business on Sunday morning, not by-laws, bake sales, or worship as entertainment. Dr. King remembered a time when the church was very powerful, a time when "early Christians rejoiced at being deemed worthy to suffer for what they believed." We were the "outside agitators" and "disturbers of the peace." Now we are tax-subsidized servants of white moderate mediocrity. King wrote:

> So often the contemporary church is a weak ineffectual voice with an uncertain sound. So often it is an arch defender of the status quo. Far from being disturbed by the presence of the church, the power structure of the average community is consoled by the church's silent—and often even vocal—sanction of things as they are. But the judgment of God is upon the church as never before. If today's church does not recapture the sacrificial spirit of the early church, it will lose its authenticity, forfeit the loyalty of millions, and be dismissed as an irrelevant social club with no meaning for the twentieth century. Every day I meet young people whose disappointment with the church has turned into outright disgust.[6]

The judgment of God is indeed upon the church, and young people are indeed disgusted with us—but this is the twenty-first century. Without resistance, without "embodied noncompliance," without The Way of Defiance, the church will continue to decline. We must believe again that we are leaven in the loaf, not peddlers of implausible doctrines. We must become again a "peculiar people," fearlessly captivated by an alternative ethic. Our task is that of a spiritual insurgency.

Just before King was assassinated, he addressed a crowd about his days in Birmingham and his battle with Bull Connor.

He said, "And then ol' Bull would say as we kept moving, 'Turn on the fire hoses,' and they did turn 'em on. But what they didn't know was that we had a fire that no water could put out."[7]

Would that the church today could stoke those fires of resistance again. Would that the waters of our baptism would make it an unquenchable fire.

Come quickly, spirit of Resistance.

Come quickly.

Amen.

Notes

1

Undone: Faith as Resistance to Ego

1. Anna Kamieńska, *Astonishments: Selected Poems of Anna Kamieńska*, ed. and trans. Grażyna Drabik and David Curzon (Brewster, MA: Paraclete Press, 2011), p. 79. Used by permission.

2. Anna Carter Florence, Professor of Preaching at Columbia Theological Seminary, used this metaphor to frame her 2012 Lyman Beecher Lectures.

3. See Fred B. Craddock, *Overhearing the Gospel* (Nashville: Abingdon, 1978).

4. Frederick Buechner, *Wishful Thinking: A Theological ABC* (New York: Harper & Row), p. 95.

5. *The Eloquence of Grace: Joseph Sittler and the Preaching Life*, ed. James M. Childs, Jr., and Richard Lischer (Eugene, OR: Cascade Books, 2012), p. 86.

6. "Teaching with Silence," an essay by the late Elaine Smokewood, Professor of English, Oklahoma City University, 2011.

7. Søren Kierkegaard, *The Point of View for My Work as an Author*, trans. Walter Lowrie (Torchbooks; New York: Harper & Row, 1962), pp. 23–24.

8. Søren Kierkegaard, *Concluding Unscientific Postscript*, trans. Walter Lowrie (Princeton, NJ: Princeton University Press, 1941), p. 222.

9. Rev. Dr. Ernest Campbell, in a lecture given at Olivet College, October 1983.

10. Doug Anderson, "Dr. Jekyll and Pastor Hyde," *Christianity Today/ Leadership Journal*, October 1, 2001.

11. Veronica Pamoukaghlian, MA, "Narcissism in High-Functioning Individuals—Big Ego or Severe Disorder?," *Psychology & Psychiatry*, November 9, 2010.

12. Anderson, "Dr. Jekyll and Pastor Hyde."

13. Ibid.

14. Ibid.

15. Ibid.

16. Peter Gomes, *The Scandalous Gospel of Jesus* (San Francisco: Harper One, 2007), p. 31.

17. Craddock, *Overhearing*, pp. 42–43.

2

Undone: Faith as Resistance to Orthodoxy

1. See Robin R. Meyers, *The Underground Church: Reclaiming the Subversive Way of Jesus* (San Francisco: Jossey-Bass, 2012).

2. Anne Lamott, *Traveling Mercies: Some Thoughts on Faith* (New York: Anchor Books, 2000), p. 22.

3. Abraham Joshua Heschel, *Essential Writings: Selected with an Introduction by Susannah Heschel* (Maryknoll, NY: Orbis Books, 2011), pp. 58–59.

4. Phyllis Tickle, *The Great Emergence: How Christianity Is Changing and Why* (Grand Rapids, MI: Baker Books, 2008), p. 16.

5. Anna Kamieńska, "Small Things," from *Astonishments: Selected Poems of Anna Kamieńska*, ed. and trans. Grażyna Drabik and David Curzon (Brewster, MA: Paraclete Press, 2011), p. 45. Used with permission.

6. Fred B. Craddock, *As One Without Authority* (Nashville: Abingdon, 1979), p. 60.

7. Fred B. Craddock, *Overhearing the Gospel* (Nashville: Abingdon, 1978), p. 83.

8. Søren Kierkegaard, *Concluding Unscientific Postscript*, trans. David Swenson and Walter Lowrie (Princeton, NJ: Princeton University Press, 1941), p. 339.

9. *There is a Fountain filled with blood.* W. Cowper. [*Passiontide*.] This hymn was probably written in 1771, as it is in Conyers's *Collection of Psalms and Hymns*, 1772.

10. Dante Gabriel Rossetti, "The Woodspurge," *Poetry X*, ed. Jough Dempsey. http://poetry.poetryx.com/poems/7106/.

11. Craddock, *As One Without Authority*, 78–81.

12. Philip Jenkins, *The Jesus Wars: How Four Patriarchs, Three Queens, and Two Emperors Decided What Christians Would Believe for the Next 1,500 Years* (San Francisco: HarperOne, 2010), pp. ix–x.

13. Ibid., p. x.

14. For the "blood of God," see Ignatius, Ephesians 1:1, in Bart Ehrman, ed. and trans., *The Apostolic Father* (Cambridge, MA: Harvard University Press, 2003), 1:219; Allen Brent, *Ignatius of Antioch* (London: T & T Clark, 2007), quoted in Jenkins, *Jesus Wars*, p. xi.

15. Jaroslav Pelikan and Valerie Hotchkiss, eds., *Creeds and Confessions of Faith in the Christian Tradition*, 4 vols. (New Haven: Yale University Press, 2003); Richard Price and Mary Whitby, eds., *Chalcedon in Context* (Liverpool: Liverpool University Press, 2009), quoted in Jenkins, *Jesus Wars*, p. xii.

16. Edward Gibbon, *The History of the Decline and Fall of the Roman Empire* (London: Henry G. Bohn, 1854), 5:2235.

17. Jenkins, *Jesus Wars*, p. xvi.

3

Undone: Faith as Resistance to Empire

1. David Sirota, "It's Time to Finally Admit We're an Empire," *AlterNet*, September 28, 2013, http://www.alternet.org/world/its-time-finally-admit-were-empire.

2. Ibid.

3. Richard Horsley, *Jesus and Empire: The Kingdom of God and the New World Disorder* (Minneapolis: Augsburg/Fortress Press, 2003), p. 54.

4. Harvey Cox, *The Future of Faith* (San Francisco: HarperOne, 2009), p. 73.

5. Ibid., p. 72.

6. John Dominic Crossan, *God and Empire: Jesus Against Rome, Then and Now* (San Francisco: HarperSanFrancisco, 2006), p. 29.

7. See Michael Hardt and Antonio Negri, *Empire* (Cambridge, MA: Harvard University Press, 2001), and *Multitude: War and Democracy in the Age of Empire* (New York: Penguin Books, 2004).

8. Crossan, *God and Empire*, p. 30.

9. Ibid., p. 28.

10. Anna Kamieńska, "Small Things," from *Astonishments: Selected Poems of Anna Kamieńska*, ed. and trans. Grażyna Drabik and David Curzon (Brewster, MA: Paraclete Press, 2011), p. 101. Used with permission.

11. Peter Gomes, *The Scandalous Gospel of Jesus* (San Francisco: Harper One, 2007), p. 177.

12. See Al Raboteau's *Slave Religion: The Invisible "Institution" in the Antebellum South* (Oxford: Oxford University Press, 2004); James Cone's *Black Theology and Black Power* (Maryknoll, NY: Orbis Books, 1997); J. Kameron Carter's *Race: A Theological Account* (Oxford: Oxford University Press, 2008); and Willie James Jennings's *The Christian Imagination: Theology and the Origins of Race* (New Haven: Yale University Press, 2011).

13. Horsley, *Jesus and Empire*, p. 56.

14. Ibid., p. 45.

15. Walter Brueggemann, *The Prophetic Imagination*, 2nd ed. (Minneapolis: Fortress Press, 2001), p. 89.

16. Horsley, *Jesus and Empire*, p. 50.

17. See Gar Alperovitz, *What Then Must We Do? Straight Talk About the Next American Revolution* (White River Junction, VT: Chelsea Green, 2013).

18. Walter Brueggemann, *Journey to the Common Good* (Louisville, KY: John Knox Press, 2010), p. 26.

19. See, by the same title, Joery Rieger and Pui-lan Kwok, *Occupy Religion: Theology of the Multitude* (Lanham, MD: Rowan & Littlefield, 2013).

20. Crossan, *God and Empire*, pp. 65–66.

Epilogue

Resisting the Reign of the Christian Status Quo

1. Robert Westbrook, "MLK's Manifesto," *The Christian Century*, April 17, 2013, p. 22.

2. Martin Luther King, Jr., *Letter from Birmingham Jail*, 1963, http://www.africa.upenn.edu/Articles_Gen/Letter_Birmingham.html.

3. Ibid.

4. See Eddie S. Glaude, Jr. *In a Shade of Blue: Pragmatism and the Politics of Black America* (Chicago: University of Chicago Press, 2008).

5. See Diana Butler Bass, *Christianity for the Rest of Us: How the Neighborhood Church Is Transforming Faith* (San Francisco: HarperOne, 2007).

6. King, *Letter from Birmingham Jail*.

7. Westbrook, "Manifesto," 27.

Index

Abernathy, Ralph, 126
Abortion, 122
Active listening, 14–15
African American churches, 106,
    109, 131
Allen, Gracie, 104
American church. *See* Church,
    American
American empire. *See* Empire
Announcements, church, 35
Anti-intellectualism, 118
Apostles' Creed, 103–104
Aristotle, 10
Artists, resistance to empire,
    98–100
Astonishments (Kamieńska), 5
Atheism, 122
Audacious act, preaching as, 1–2,
    13–14, 31

Baptism, 57–58, 103
Beecher, Henry Ward, xii
Beecher, Lyman, xii
Beecher (Lyman) Lectures,
    Yale University: angst of
    speaker, 2–3; audience for,

3; of Craddock (1978), 9;
    ego of speaker, 2, 19–20;
    establishment of, xii;
    qualifications of invitee, xii;
    as rhetorical events, xix;
    simulcast, xix–xx; subject
    matter of, xii–xiii
Berry, Wendell, 107
Blake, William, 23
Brooks, Phillips, 21
Brueggemann, Walter, 92,
    107, 114
Buechner, Frederick, 10–11
Burwell v. Hobby Lobby, 95

Caesar, tribute to, 110–111
Campbell, Ernest, 22, 103–104
Camus, Albert, 43
Capitalism, and empire, 95
Centered self, 14
Certainty, resistance to, 45–46,
    74–75
Chalcedon, council at, 72
Chesterton, G. K., xiv
Chosen people, 60
Christian Right, xi–xii

Church, American: African
American churches, 106, 109,
131; and civil rights movement,
125–130, 133–134; courageous
congregations, 130–131; decline
of, x–xviii, 48–49, 54–55, 133;
government subsidies to,
89–90, 113; growth of
orthodoxy, 63–65; qualities of
thriving congregations, 132;
renewal of, 113–124, 132–134;
separation of church and state,
114–115; spiritual fatigue in, 100;
status quo supported by, 85, 90,
91–92, 102–103, 107–108,
126–129, 132; and war, 97–98; as
white refuge, 116. *See also*
Ministry; Personality styles,
clerical; Preaching
*Citizens United v. Federal Election
Commission*, 95, 119
Civil rights movement, 109, 125–130
Climate change, 107, 117–118
"Clod and the Pebble, The"
(Blake), 23
Coffin, William Sloane, Jr., 2,
94, 118
Comma, in life of Jesus, 103–104
Community organizing, 115
Concept and capacity, 45, 55
Connor, Bull, 133–134
Connotative/denotative meanings,
38–39
Constantine, Emperor, 89
Corley, Kathleen, 86–87
Cox, Harvey, 92
Craddock, Fred B., xiii, 9, 15, 53–54,
66, 67
Crossan, John Dominic, 96–97
Cross symbol, 85, 86

Crucifixion victims, funeral rituals
for, 87
Cult of the Dead, 87

Debt, cancellation of, 120–121
Deductive preaching, 53–54
Denotative/connotative meanings,
38–39
Depressive clerical personality
type, 27, 30, 37
Distributive justice, 120
Doubt, 46–47
Dyer, Mark, 48
Dylan, Bob, 10

Egan, Timothy, 4
Ego-bound *v.* free man, 45
Ego-involvement, clerical, 19–22,
30, 33–34, 35–36
Emergent movement, 131
Empire, xviii, 18, 42; artists'
resistance to, 98–100; capitalism
as, 95; church communities in
resistance to, 130–131; church
conformity to status quo, 85,
90, 90–91, 102, 107–108, 126–129,
132; church renewal as
resistance to, 113–124; and
church/state relations, 89–90,
114–115; definition of, 93; as
domination systems within
ourselves, 92–93; illusion about,
81–82; Jesus People's resistance
to, 81, 84, 86–88, 96–97; Jesus's
resistance to, 81, 101, 106–107,
109–113; leaking secrets of, 112;
mass media, 93–95; preaching
as resistance to, 104–106;
premises of, 83, 91; proof of,
81–83; and war, 95–96, 97–98

Environmental destruction,
    107–108

Faith: meaning of, 44–48;
    misconceptions about, 50–51; as
    resistance, xviii, 7, 18, 41–42, 85;
    science and, xv; socially
    responsible, 105; trust and, 36;
    as truth, 75
Faith-based initiatives, 113
Fish, sign of, 84–85
Flag, displayed in churches, 90, 113
Florence, Anna Carter, 8
Fonteyn, Margot, 19
Fountain Street church, Grand
    Rapids, 130
Francis, Pope, 105, 122
Fromm, Erich, 45

Gay rights, 43, 98, 121–122, 129
Gibbon, Edward, 72–73
Gomes, Peter J., 32–33
Good Shepherd UCC, Sahuarita,
    Arizona, 130
Grace, 17
Grandiose clerical personality
    type, 23–25, 29, 36
Guthrie, Woody, 32

Heresy, orthodoxy and, 76
Herod, 106
Heschel, Abraham Joshua, 46
The History of the Decline and Fall
    of the Roman Empire (Gibbon),
    72–73
Horsley, Richard, 81, 91, 106–107
Hosea, 107

Idolatry, 17
Ignatius, 71

Immigration, illegal, 121
Incarnation, 66–67
Individualism, hyper-, xiv
Intellectual dishonesty, 67
Iraq, invasion of, 97–98
Isaiah, 105

Jenkins, Philip, 67–68, 71
Jesus: Chamber of Commerce, 116;
    claims about, 51; divine
    evolution of, 69–71; dual nature
    of, 71–73; explanations v.
    experience of, 47; first sermon
    preached by, 104–105; parables
    of, 17; resistance to empire, 81,
    101, 106–107, 109–113; resistance
    to orthodoxy, 55–63
Jesus People: common ownership
    of land, 85; as community of
    defiance, xiii–xiv, 6–7, 42, 84;
    resistance to empire, 84, 86–88,
    96–97; in spiritual collectives, 84
Jesus Wars, The (Jenkins), 67–68
John, gospel of, 68–69, 70
"Joys and concerns" group sharing,
    35
Judson Memorial Church, New
    York City, 130

Kamieńska, Anna, 79; "Small
    Things," 52–53;
    "Transformation," 5–6, 28–31;
    "The Weariness of the Prophet
    Elijah," 99–100
Keck, Leander, 75
Keystone XL pipeline protest, 18
Kierkegaard, Søren, xi, xv, 15, 63,
    92, 94; on illusion, 54, 93; on
    loss of passion, 35; on
    undoneness, 2, 9, 17, 45

King, Martin Luther, Jr., 8, 91, 106,
     131; on church decline, 133; on
     church resistance, 128–130,
     133–134; in historical context,
     108–109; *Letter from
     Birmingham Jail*, 125–128

Lamott, Anne, 43
Leopold, Aldo, 107
Letter from Birmingham Jail
     (King), 125–128
Lewis, C. S., 45
Listening, active, 14–15

Manning, Bradley, 112
March on Washington, 119
Mark, gospel of, 60, 69, 70, 108,
     109–110
Mass media empire, 93–95
Mayflower Congregational UCC,
     4–5, 28
McKibben, Bill, 107
Meyers, Robin: as academic, xiii;
     background and upbringing of,
     3–4; invitation to give Beecher
     Lecture, xii, 2–3; length of
     pastorate, 28; vocation of, 21
Military bases, 82
Military expenditures, 83
Ministry: as career, 8–9, 12, 22;
     in dying church, x; long
     pastorates, 27–28; marketing of,
     16, 47–48, 49–50, 102–103, 104;
     as performance, xvi, 18, 21, 45;
     social gospel, 90, 102, 130–131; as
     subject of Beecher Lectures,
     xii–xiii; as vocation, 10–13,
     21–22. *See also* Personality
     styles, clerical; Preaching
Monophysites, 72

Moral imagination, xiv–xv, 37
Moral March Movement, 131
Muir, John, 107

Narcissistic/grandiose clerical
     personality type, 23–25, 29, 36
New York Times, 117
Nicean Creeds, 64–65, 89

Obama, Barack, xi–xii, 82, 117
Occupy movement, 127
Oklahoma: fracking in, 32;
     Keystone XL pipeline protest
     in, 18; pioneering people of, 3–4
Orthodoxy, xviii, 18, 42; and
     certainty, 45–46, 74–75;
     conformity to, 76–79;
     contradictions of, 67–68; and
     decline of church, 48–55; and
     divinity of Jesus, 69–71; and dual
     nature of Jesus, 71–73; ethical,
     80; growth of, 63–65; as heretical,
     76; Jesus's resistance to, 55–63;
     and meaning of faith, 44–48
Orwell, George, 94
Othering, 34

Paul, 70, 101, 120
Perfectionist clerical personality
     type, 25–27, 29, 37
Personality styles: clerical, 22–23;
     depressive, 27, 30, 37; grandiose/
     narcissistic, 23–25, 29, 36;
     perfectionist, 25–27, 29, 37
Plymouth Congregational UCC,
     Washington, D.C., 130–131
Poetry reading, 29
Preaching: and active listening,
     14–15; audacity of, 1–2, 13–14, 31;
     authenticity of, 13–14;

avoidance of politics, 101;
celebrity preachers, 15–16;
credibility of, 12–13; deductive,
53–54; ego-involvement in,
19–22, 30, 33–34, 35–36; and fear
of offending, 31–34, 36; loss of
passion, 34–35; ordinary time,
34; of "prosperity gospel," 64; as
resistance, 104–106; task of,
9–10; with tracing paper, 78–79.
See also Ministry; Personality
styles, clerical
Privacy, loss of, 92

Rand, Ayn, 32
Rauschenbusch, Walter, 90
Reagan, Ronald, 98
Redemptive violence, 91
Relevance of church, xv–xvi
Repentance, 13
"Repertory Church," 8
Resistance: defined, 6–10, 42–43; to
ego (*See* Ministry; Personality
styles, clerical; Preaching); to
empire (*See* Empire); forms of,
18, 42; to orthodoxy (*See*
Orthodoxy)
Resurrection, 70
Righteous warfare, language of,
43–44
Rilke, Rainer Maria, 45
Riverside Cathedral, New York
City, 130
Riverside Church of Christ,
Wichita, Kansas, 4
Rohr, Richard, 1
Rollins, Peter, 41
Roman Catholic Church, 128, 131
Roman empire: Christian dissident
movement in, 84, 86–88; Jesus's

resistance to, 81, 101, 106–107,
109–113; official religion of, 89;
premises of, 83
Rossetti, Dante Gabriel, "The
Woodspurge," 65–66
Rummage sale metaphor, 48–49

Sabbath, 61, 107, 113–114
Sage, Henry, xii
Salvation, 7
Science, and faith, xv
Separation of church and state,
114–115
Sermon on the Mount, 103
Sittler, Joseph, 11–12
"Small Things" (Kamieńska),
52–53
Snowden, Edward, 112
Social gospel ministry, 90, 102, 131
Social network, xiv, 92
Social responsibility, 90, 105
Socrates, 16
Son of God, 69–71
Sovereignty, transfer of, ix
Stewart, Jon, 113
Stowe, Harriet Beecher, xii

Taxes: church deductions, 89, 113;
Jesus's resistance to, 110–111
Taylor, Barbara Brown, 75
"Teaching with Silence," 14
Thatcher, Margaret, 98
Theology. *See* Orthodoxy
"This land is your land," 32
Tickle, Phyllis, 48
Tillich, Paul, 14
Time, myth of, 128
"Transformation" (Kamieńska),
5–6, 28–31
Trust, 27–28, 36

Undone and undoing, 6, 7, 9, 17,
    39, 45, 124
Unintended consequences, 67
United Church of Christ, 4–5, 104,
    121, 130–131
University Congregational UCC,
    Seattle, 131

Vietnam, connotative meaning of
    word, 38–39

Wallace, George, 127
War: empire's deception about,
    95–96, 97–98; opposition to, 36;

preemptive, 82; redemptive
    violence, 91
Warburton, William, 76
"Weariness of the Prophet Elijah,
    The" (Kamieńska), 99–100
Weaver, Richard, 93
"Who do people say that I am?"
    question, of Jesus, 66–69, 72
Wink, Walter, 98
Women: equality of, 43, 121;
    resistance to Rome, 87
"Wordspurge, The" (Rosetti),
    65–66
Worship, as act of resistance, 8